NICK GROSSO

Sweetheart

faber and faber

LONDON · BOSTON

First published in 1996
by Faber and Faber Limited
3 Queen Square London WC1N 3AU

Nick Grosso is hereby identified as author of this
work in accordance with Section 77 of the Copyright,
Designs and Patents Act 1988

A CIP record for this book
is available from the British Library

ISBN 0–571–17967–3

2 4 6 8 10 9 7 5 3 1

Characters

Charlie
Ruby
Friend 1
Friend 2
Steve
Toni
Davey
Kelly
Lee
Man

Apart from Steve and the Man all the characters are from north London and in their early–mid-twenties. The action takes place over a period of two weeks.

This text went to press before the opening night and may therefore differ from the version as performed

Sweetheart was first performed at the Royal Court Theatre Upstairs on 25 January 1996 with the following cast:

Toni Kate Beckinsale
Charlie Joe Duttine
Ruby Diane Parish
Davey/Man Darren Tighe
Kelly Nicola Walker
Lee/Steve Rick Warden

Directed by Roxana Silbert
Designed by David Roger
Lighting Designed by Mark Ridler
Sound Designed by Paul Arditti

First Part

SCENE ONE

NW1. HQ'S Nightclub. Friday. 1.00 a.m. Dance music in the background. Bottles of beer. **Ruby** *and two girlfriends exit the ladies just as* **Charlie** *exits the gents.*

Charlie Hi ruby.

Ruby Oh hiya!

Charlie Hi.

Ruby Hi.

Charlie How's it going?

Ruby Okay.

Charlie I haven't seen you in years.

Ruby I know.

Charlie How's it going?

Ruby Okay.

Pause.

Charlie How's it going?

Ruby Okay.

Charlie It's funny you know.

Ruby What is?

Charlie I'm telling ya.

Ruby What?

Charlie I was talking about you today.

Ruby Were you?

Charlie Yeah.

Ruby Really?

Charlie Yeah.

Ruby With who?

Charlie I saw rachel on the tube.

Ruby Did you? How is she?

Charlie She's okay. I was sitting opposite her for ages then i thought 'shit that's wotsherface innit' – i couldn't remember her name.

Ruby Rachel.

Charlie Yeah. I know. I thought about it for two stops and then i remembered.

Charlie and Ruby Rachel.

Charlie Yeah. So i leans forward and she thinks i'm about to rape her.

Ruby laughs.

You know what she's like. She's about to swipe me with her big issue dya know what i mean?

Ruby Didn't she recognize you?

Charlie No.

Ruby That's surprising.

Charlie I know. So i go 'excuse me …'.

Ruby's friends confer.

'Aren't you rachel?'.

Friend 1 (*quietly*) Ruby we're going inside.

Ruby Okay.

Ruby's friends walk off.

Charlie Shit i'm not butting in am i?

Ruby No.

Charlie We weren't rude?

Ruby They'll never talk to me again.

Charlie Stroppy cows.

They laugh.

Are they your friends?

Ruby Yeah.

Charlie I didn't mean … i'm sure they're … nice people.

Ruby They are.

Charlie They could learn some manners.

Ruby They're from broken homes.

Charlie It shows.

They laugh.

So i goes …

Ruby Yeah.

Charlie 'Are you rachel?'.

Ruby Yeah.

Charlie And she goes 'yeah' … she don't recognize me though.

Ruby That's surprising.

Charlie I know. So i says '*it's charlie* …'.

Ruby laughs.

And she chills and we chat and that and she asks if i ever see you.

Ruby Does she?

Charlie Yeah. So i say 'no' – not since you split up with … anyway …

Ruby laughs coyly.

I explained it all to her don't worry.

Ruby laughs coyly.

So she says if i see you to say hello but i said there was fat chance of that but she said if i did so i said okay and then what dya know i see ya here on the *very same fucking day after all these years*! (*He shakes his head in wonder.*) Unbelievable.

Ruby How is she?

Charlie Oh ya know.

Ruby What's she doing?

Charlie She's a research assistant or something.

Ruby Is she?

Charlie For some TV firm … everyone's in TV these days have ya noticed?

Ruby I know.

Charlie It's a scandal. What do you do?

Ruby I'm a casting assistant.

Charlie What?

Ruby laughs.

Ruby A casting assistant.

Charlie What's that?

Ruby I assist casting.

Charlie Do ya?

Ruby nods.

What's that then?

Ruby Well you know how you might have a guinness commercial.

Charlie Yeah.

Ruby And there's all those ordinary people on the street saying why they like guinness.

Charlie No i musta missed that one.

Ruby No i'm just saying … for instance.

Charlie Oh yeah.

They laugh.

Ruby Well i find those people.

Pause.

Charlie You find those people?

Ruby Yeah.

Charlie That's your job?

Ruby Yeah.

Charlie Shit.

Ruby It's not that easy … you have to find the right people with the right faces and the right voices … and the right 'feel' about them … it's not that easy.

5

Charlie Shit.

Ruby laughs.

So where dya find these people?

Ruby We look them up on our files ... or we phone around ... and ask people ... you know.

Charlie You mean actors?

Ruby No.

Charlie What?

Ruby Real people.

Charlie What – you mean you use *real* people?

Ruby Yeah.

Charlie What – like me?

Ruby Yeah.

Charlie Shit ... i always thought they were actors.

Ruby shakes her head.

Pretending to be real. Shit ... you serious?

Ruby Yeah.

Charlie Well i tell ya what.

Ruby What?

Charlie They're good ... i mean i always thought they were actors.

Pause.

Ruby It's funny you know.

Charlie What is?

Ruby Well ... i was thinking about *you* too.

Charlie Was ya?

Ruby nods.

When?

Ruby The other day.

Charlie How come?

Ruby Tony was talking about you.

Charlie Was he?

Ruby nods.

Dya still see him?

Ruby Now and then.

Charlie I never knew … you broke his heart you know.

Ruby laughs coyly.

No i mean …

Ruby laughs coyly.

I'm not saying nothing, i mean …

Ruby laughs coyly

I'm just saying.

Ruby Did *he* say that?

Charlie Nah you're joking … not tone … he'd never say that.

Ruby How dya know then?

Charlie You could tell.

Ruby Could you?

Charlie Well *i* could.

Ruby How?

Charlie B/cos ... you know ...

Ruby That's the thing about tone ...

Charlie What?

Ruby He won't confront his feelings.

Charlie looks bemused.

Charlie What?

Ruby He's quite a closed person.

Charlie Is he?

Ruby Don't ya reckon?

Charlie ponders.

Charlie Dunno ... he's my mate.

Ruby He's quite a closed person.

Pause.

Charlie What was he saying?

Ruby looks at Charlie inquiringly.

About me.

Ruby Oh ya know ... what you were doing.

Charlie Yeah?

Ruby Yeah.

Charlie Don't believe him.

Ruby Why?

Charlie He lies.

Ruby You don't know what he said!

Charlie He spices everything up.

Ruby Does he?

Charlie Yeah … to make himself look … 'exotic'.

They laugh.

Ruby He could never look exotic.

Charlie What?

Ruby Not tone … when i was going out with him …
sonia said i'd become boring.

Charlie What?

Ruby Yeah.

Charlie *Sonia*!?

Ruby Yeah.

Charlie Shit. That's rich.

Ruby laughs.

Cheeky bitch.

Ruby She was right though.

Charlie Was she … ? Nah.

Ruby She was.

Pause.

Charlie Nah.

Ruby I was so shy then don't you remember?

Charlie Not really.

Ruby You must.

Charlie I didn't really know you.

Ruby That's the thing about tone …

Charlie What?

Ruby He always kept his friends at a distance.

Charlie Did he?

Ruby Yeah.

Charlie Nah. Not tone.

Ruby He did.

Pause.

Charlie That's just b/cos he loved you.

Pause.

Ruby You know …

Pause.

Charlie What?

Ruby Well …

Pause.

Charlie What?

Ruby You were the only one of his friends …

Pause.

Charlie Yeah … ?

Ruby I could talk to.

Pause.

Charlie Was i?

Ruby You were always friendly to me.

Charlie Was i?

Ruby You were never intimidating.

Charlie looks bemused.

Charlie Why should i be?

Ruby shrugs.

Ruby Dunno … you know people like jake … ?

Charlie Yeah.

Ruby He always made me feel weird.

Charlie Weird?

Ruby Yeah ya know … uncomfortable.

Pause.

Charlie He only projected that image.

Ruby I know.

Charlie Cos *he* felt weird. He *is* weird.

Ruby laughs.

He's a fucking weirdo i tell ya.

Ruby laughs.

I bet he was intimidated by *you*.

Ruby What?

Charlie *Course*. He was in love with you.

Ruby What?

Charlie *Course* … who wouldn't be?

Ruby laughs coyly.

I mean …

Ruby I was so shy in those days.

Charlie I know.

Ruby looks surprised.

You said.

Ruby laughs.

What changed?

Ruby shrugs.

Ruby I've just got more confidence.

Charlie Have you?

Ruby nods.

How come?

Ruby shrugs.

It's funny.

Ruby What is?

Charlie Well ... i can't remember ever really talking to you.

Ruby That's b/cos i was shy.

Charlie Yeah i know but you said ...

Ruby What?

Charlie You said i was the only one of tone's friends ...

Ruby I meant you were the only one of his friends i *wanted* to talk to.

Charlie nods.

Charlie I get it.

Pause.

Ruby I had a dream about you.

Charlie Did you?

Ruby nods.

When?

Ruby The other day.

Pause.

Charlie Shit.

Ruby You were sitting on a bus …

Charlie Was i?

Ruby nods.

Which one?

Ruby Two-five-four.

Charlie Upstairs or downstairs?

Ruby Upstairs. By the window.

Charlie thinks back.

Charlie What day?

Ruby laughs.

What happened?

Ruby I was standing in the street and as the bus went by i saw you so i shouted your name but you never heard me so i shouted louder and louder but … (*She shrugs defeatedly.*)

Charlie I'm a bit deaf in one ear.

Ruby laughs.

What dya think it means?

Ruby I dunno … i guess it means i've been thinking

about you … i've been thinking about that whole scene really … we were so young … i guess i thought if you got to know me …

Pause.

Charlie Yeah … ?

Ruby You wouldn't *want* to know me.

Charlie Shit.

Ruby It's silly.

Charlie shakes his head in wonder.

Charlie That's unbelievable.

Pause.

Ruby Are you still going out with toni?

Charlie Yeah.

Pause.

Ruby It's funny innit?

Charlie What is?

Ruby Well … i went out with tony and …

Pause.

Charlie Yeah.

They laugh.

Tony's an ambidextrous name.

They laugh. Pause.

What about you?

Ruby Boyfriends?

Charlie Yeah.

Ruby I'm all over the place at the moment.

Charlie Are you?

   Ruby nods.

Why?

Ruby I've got two.

   Charlie looks startled.

Charlie *Two*!?

   Ruby laughs coyly.

Ruby They're both older than me.

Charlie Are they?

Ruby They're father figures.

Charlie Shit.

Ruby One of them's alright though.

Charlie What about the other one?

Ruby Barry … ?

   Charlie shrugs.

He's a creep.

Charlie So why … ?

Ruby He's a TV producer.

   Charlie nods.

Charlie I see.

Ruby Well not a producer … an executive.

Charlie What's that?

Ruby He's got lots of contacts.

Charlie Right.

Ruby I wanna be a newsreader.

Charlie Do ya?

Ruby Yeah. He's heard my voice and he likes it.

They laugh.

Charlie So how dya meet?

Ruby In a bar ... he was with another woman ... leggy model type ... you know ... i didn't fancy him i thought he was a creep.

Charlie looks at Ruby dubiously.

Charlie So what happened?

Ruby He followed me home.

Charlie What!?

Ruby He jumped on my tube and sat beside me ... he said he'd been watching me all night and he *had* to talk to me.

Charlie What did he say?

Ruby thinks back.

Ruby He said what he did and everything ... then he asked what *i* did ... then he asked me what my dreams were.

Charlie Your dreams?

Ruby Yeah.

Charlie That's a bit personal.

Ruby I know. So i said i wanna be a newsreader.

Charlie And?

Ruby He said he could get me on radio chiltern.

Charlie What's that?

Ruby It's a radio station.

Charlie Where?

Ruby In chiltern i suppose.

Charlie Where's that?

Ruby ponders.

Ruby Dunno … somewhere in the regions.

Charlie nods.

Charlie So what did *you* say?

Ruby I said i'd think about it … then he asked me out.

Charlie looks at Ruby inquiringly.

I said no.

Charlie *Good* … and … ?

Ruby He got off at my stop and ran after me.

Charlie looks startled.

Charlie What dya do?

Ruby I told him to stop.

Charlie looks at Ruby inquiringly.

He said only if i gave him my number.

Charlie So … ?

Ruby So i gave it to him.

Charlie looks startled.

Charlie What!?

Ruby laughs coyly.

You gave him your number!?

Ruby Yeah.

Charlie *Why!?*

Ruby shrugs.

Ruby I suppose i was curious.

Pause.

Charlie So now he's your boyfriend?

Blackout.

SCENE TWO

NW8. Ruby's bedroom. Friday. 3.00 a.m. Bob Marley in the background. Cups of tea. Charlie is lying on the futon. Ruby is sitting on it.

Charlie It's cold in here.

Ruby Is it?

Charlie Yeah. Aren't you cold?

Ruby Not really. I'm used to it.

Charlie How come?

Ruby The heating's gone.

Charlie Great.

Ruby Steve's taken it apart.

Charlie Who's steve?

Ruby My mum's boyfriend.

Charlie Is he a plumber?

Ruby He's a buffoon.

Charlie looks surprised.

Charlie That's nice.

Ruby I know.

Charlie Don't you get on?

Ruby Not really. He's an architect.

Charlie nods.

Charlie Oh.

Ruby He's always changing things.

Charlie Like what?

Ruby Like the radiators ... he's obsessed with the way things *look* ... like if you're upstairs ... or you're downstairs say and you take a chair from upstairs ... you have to take it *back* before he sees it or he flips.

Charlie Shit.

Ruby He literally has *spasms* ... it drives me *spare* ... and he makes things.

Charlie What things?

Ruby Things we don't need.

Charlie Like what?

Ruby Like i dunno ... french windows.

Charlie What's those?

Ruby Windows they have in france ... he made some for the lounge.

Charlie That's nice.

Ruby looks surprised.

Ruby What?

Charlie It's nice to make things.

Ruby Is it?

Charlie We all need people to make things.

Ruby Why?

Charlie shrugs.

Charlie I dunno ... so *we* don't have to.

Ruby But we don't *need* french windows.

Charlie So?

Ruby Who does?

Charlie That's not the point ... you don't make things cos you *need* em do ya.

Ruby Don't ya?

Charlie No ... ! You make cos you *wanna* ... it's like life.

Ruby Why you on his side?

Charlie I'm not.

Ruby You are.

Charlie He's your mum's boyfriend.

Ruby So?

Charlie So ... you should like his windows.

Ruby Why?

Charlie Cos he made them himself.

Ruby shrugs.

Ruby That don't mean i have to like them.

Charlie It does ... have *you* ever made something?

Ruby Yeah.

Charlie What?

Ruby looks around the room. She points.

Ruby That painting.

Charlie looks at the painting.

Charlie You did that?

Ruby Yeah.

Pause.

Charlie When?

Ruby When i was at school.

Pause.

Charlie Right.

Ruby Dya like it?

Charlie looks at the painting.

Charlie What is it?

Ruby Have a guess.

Charlie looks at the painting.

Charlie Dunno.

Ruby It's an urban landscape.

Charlie looks at the painting.

Charlie Shit.

Ruby It's abstract.

Charlie I thought it was.

Ruby It is.

Charlie I like the colours.

Ruby Do ya?

Charlie Yeah … it reminds me …

Ruby What?

Charlie Of tony's paintings.

   Pause.

Ruby I knew you'd say that.

Charlie Well it does.

   Pause.

Ruby He encouraged me.

Charlie Did he?

Ruby Yeah.

Charlie It shows.

Ruby He taught me how to do tone.

Charlie Tone?

Ruby Yeah ya know …

Charlie What – tone did?

Ruby Yeah.

   They laugh.

He's ambidextrous.

   They laugh. Pause.

Charlie He's a good teacher.

Ruby Thanks.

Pause.

Charlie He's a good painter.

Ruby Dya reckon?

Charlie Course ... don't you?

Ruby I suppose.

Pause.

Charlie What?

Ruby Nothing. (*Pause.*) He's talented.

Pause.

Charlie But?

Ruby I find his paintings a bit ... eclectic.

Charlie Eclectic?

Ruby nods.

What's that?

Ruby Don't you know?

Charlie No.

Ruby Well ... say a painting's all blue say ...

Charlie Yeah.

Ruby Or all green.

Charlie Yeah.

Ruby Well ... eclectic's the opposite of that.

Charlie looks bemused.

Charlie So you'd rather his paintings were all one colour?

Ruby No.

Charlie What then?

Ruby Not necessarily.

Pause.

Charlie What then?

Ruby shrugs.

Ruby I dunno.

Pause.

Charlie It's cold.

Ruby There's a heater downstairs.

Charlie Is there?

Ruby I'll get it.

Ruby starts to move but Charlie tugs her back.

Charlie Nah don't bother.

Ruby Why?

Charlie Don't bother. (*Pause.*) Maybe you could close the window.

Ruby gets up and closes the window.

What's your mum's boyfriend called?

Ruby Steve.

Charlie Why'd he mess up the heating?

Ruby sits on the futon.

Ruby He wants to install new radiators.

Charlie Does he?

Ruby nods.

Why?

Ruby B/cos he's an idiot i told you … he says these ones are 'un-aesthetic'.

Charlie What?

Ruby They don't look nice.

Charlie They look fine.

Ruby He's gonna get cast iron ones … made of …

Charlie and Ruby Cast iron.

Ruby Yeah … they cost an absolute *bomb*.

Charlie Shit.

Ruby I try telling mum … but … she says she's happy if he's happy.

Charlie Well then.

Ruby That's what she always says.

Pause.

Charlie Why dya hate him?

Ruby looks surprised.

Ruby I don't.

Charlie You do.

Pause.

Ruby He gives me the creeps.

Charlie Why?

Ruby No reason.

Charlie looks at Ruby dubiously.

When we have breakfast ... he kisses me.

Charlie What?

Ruby chuckles coyly.

Where?

Ruby In the kitchen.

Charlie How?

Pause.

Ruby Like that.

Ruby pecks Charlie on the cheek.

Charlie When?

Ruby Before he goes to work.

Pause.

Charlie So?

Pause.

Ruby Nothing.

Charlie Does he kiss your mum?

Ruby Yeah.

Charlie Well then.

Ruby What?

Charlie He's just being friendly.

Ruby shakes her head.

Ruby He's not.

Charlie He is ... it's normal.

Ruby shakes her head.

Ruby It ain't.

Charlie Well tell him.

Ruby I can't.

Charlie Why not?

Ruby B/cos ... if i did ... i'd make it an issue.

Charlie It *is* an issue.

Ruby I know.

Charlie So?

Ruby I dunno ... i'd hurt his feelings.

Charlie Fuck his feelings.

Ruby I can't.

Charlie Why not?

Ruby He's not a bad person.

Charlie sighs.

Charlie Well let him.

Ruby I can't.

Charlie Well tell him.

Ruby I can't.

Pause.

Charlie Well tell your mum.

Ruby shakes her head.

Why not?

Ruby She loves him.

Pause.

Charlie Well skip breakfast.

Pause.

Ruby There's something else.

Charlie What?

Ruby When i go to bed ... i kiss him goodnight.

Charlie Why?

Ruby I have to.

Charlie looks startled.

Well i don't *have* to ... it's a sorta ... ritual ... i say good-night ... i kiss mum ... (*She cringes.*) and then i kiss him.

Charlie Why?

Ruby You know ...

Charlie No.

Ruby Otherwise it'd be obvious.

Charlie What would?

Ruby That i hadn't kissed him.

Charlie So?

Ruby shrugs.

Ruby I dunno.

Charlie Don't kiss him.

Ruby I know ... you're right ... i've done it for so long now ... i'm trapped.

Charlie Shit.

Ruby It gives me the creeps.

Charlie I'm not surprised.

Ruby looks surprised.

Ruby Dya reckon?

Charlie Yeah.

Ruby But you said ...

Charlie What?

Ruby You said *him* kissing *me* was normal.

Charlie It *is*.

Ruby Why?

Charlie That's in the morning ... over brekkie ... this night shit ... (*He shakes his head disapprovingly.*) That's weird.

There is a knock at the door. Ruby jumps up and runs towards it but it opens immediately. **Steve** *appears and stands inside the doorway. He is in pyjamas. Ruby freezes. Steve looks at Charlie then Ruby.*

Ruby Steve.

Pause.

Steve Ruby.

Pause.

Ruby Steve.

Pause.

Steve Ruby ... do you know what time it is?

Ruby looks round at the clock.

Ruby Three o'clock.

Steve It's three o'clock.

Pause.

Ruby I'm sorry.

Steve We're trying to sleep.

Ruby I'm sorry.

Steve Don't you have work tomorrow?

Ruby nods.

Well?

Ruby We were just talking. (*She turns round at Charlie.*) This is charlie.

Charlie nods.

(*to Charlie*) Steve.

Steve Hi.

Charlie Hi. (*Pause.*) Nice house you got here. (*He clears his throat.*) Lovely windows.

Steve Thanks … (*to Ruby*) Could you turn the music down?

Ruby nods.

Please.

Ruby Okay.

Steve And your voices.

Ruby nods. Steve spots their shoes lying on the floor. He sighs.

What have i said about shoes?

Ruby What?

Steve I've told you … you leave them in the hallway … we don't want footprints scraping the floorboards do we?

Ruby No.

Steve No ... we don't ... it took an age to do those floor-boards.

Ruby I know.

Steve We don't want you spoiling them.

Ruby collects the shoes.

Give them to me.

Ruby gives Steve the shoes.

I'll take them.

Ruby Thanks.

Steve But ruby?

Ruby What?

Pause.

Steve Please try to remember.

Ruby I will.

Steve nods.

Steve Goodnight.

Ruby Goodnight.

Steve glances at Charlie and exits. He closes the door quietly. Ruby stares at the door. She turns to face Charlie.

(*whispers*) *Shit*!

Charlie shakes his head in wonder.

(*whispers*) Dya think he heard us?

Charlie (*whispers*) What?

Ruby (*whispers*) Dya think he heard what we were saying?

Charlie ponders.

Charlie (*whispers*) Dunno.

Ruby (*whispers*) Oh my *god*!

They laugh quietly. Ruby turns off the stereo.

Charlie You should get outa here.

Ruby I know ... i want to but i can't afford it.

Charlie But you're earning.

Ruby shrugs defeatedly.

Ruby But i'm a spendthrift.

They laugh.

Dya wanna hear my news reports?

Charlie What?

Ruby plays a cassette of her reading a news bulletin. Charlie looks bemused.

Ruby Barry helped me do it.

Charlie Who's barry?

Ruby The executive ... remember?

Charlie Oh yeah.

Ruby His friend's got a studio.

Charlie Has he?

Ruby In the country.

Charlie Great.

Ruby It was such fun ... anyway.

Ruby exits. Charlie shakes his head in wonder. He gets up and strips down to his underwear and gets into bed.

Ruby enters holding a toothbrush and beaker. She sits astride him and gently brushes both their teeth in alternate strokes. They rinse their mouths and spit into the beaker. Ruby puts the toothbrush and beaker down. She puts her mouth to Charlie's. They smooch. Charlie pushes her away.

What's the matter?

Charlie This is weird.

Ruby Why?

Charlie You know.

Pause.

Ruby Tony?

Pause.

Charlie It just feels …

Pause.

Ruby What?

Charlie Like this is his territory.

Ruby It's no-one's territory.

Charlie It is.

Pause.

Ruby You mean it's contraband?

Charlie What?

Ruby Contraband.

Charlie What's that?

Ruby You don't know?

Charlie No.

Ruby You haven't got a very good vocabulary.

Charlie What's that?

Ruby laughs.

Ruby Vocabulary?

Charlie What's that?

Ruby You must know what vocabulary is!

Charlie What's that?

Ruby It means you don't know any words.

Charlie What's that?

Ruby It means you're thick.

Charlie stares at Ruby reproachfully.

Charlie What's that?

Blackout.

SCENE THREE

NW5. **Toni***'s bedroom. Sunday. 5.00 p.m. Futon bed. Toni is asleep. A nurse's uniform hangs. Charlie walks on in a pair of boxers. He is drying his hair with a towel.*

Charlie Toni. (*Pause.*) Toni. (*Pause.*) Wake up.

Toni grunts.

Toni.

Toni grunts.

Toni.

Toni *What*!?

Charlie It's time to get up sweetheart ... it's five o'clock. (*Pause.*) Toni.

Toni raises her head.

Toni Yeah ... !?

Charlie It's time to get up.

Toni rubs her eyes.

Toni No it's not.

Toni's head hits the pillow.

Charlie It is sweetheart ... come on.

Toni Leave me alone.

Charlie Come on sweetheart. (*Pause.*) Toni.

Toni raises her head.

Toni *What*!?

Charlie I told you ... ! We'll be late.

Toni For what?

Charlie The picnic.

Toni groans.

Toni Who cares?

Charlie They do.

Pause.

Toni No they don't.

Charlie They do ... you know they do.

Toni sighs.

They'll be waiting.

Toni They won't.

Charlie They will ... we're always late for things.

Toni So *what*?

Charlie So we said we'd be there at four ... it's now five.

Toni's head hits the pillow.

Come on sweetheart.

Toni Then go.

Charlie What?

Toni Go.

Charlie What dya mean?

Toni I'll see you there later.

Charlie I can't go by myself.

Toni Why not?

Charlie B/cos i can't ... toni.

Toni raises her head.

Toni *What*!?

Charlie You gotta come.

Toni Why?

Charlie B/cos they're *your* friends.

Toni They're *your* friends.

Charlie No they're not.

Toni They are.

Charlie They're not ... not properly ... besides ...

Toni What?

Charlie You said you'd come.

Toni No i never.

Charlie You did.

Toni When?

Charlie Yesterday ... in the kitchen ... remember?

Toni No.

Charlie You said you'd be back early and ...

Toni So?

Charlie You said you'd come!

Toni I said if i *felt* like it.

Charlie What ... ? No you never!

Toni I did!

Charlie You never!

Toni How would you *know* charlie?

Charlie What?

Toni You don't *listen* ... ! You don't *listen* charlie.

   Pause.

Charlie What the fuck ... !?

Toni I'm tired!

Charlie I know!

Toni *Do you*!?

Charlie *Yes* ... ! I do ... you're always fucking tired.

   Pause.

Toni That's b/cos ...

Charlie and Toni I work!

Charlie I know!

Toni I *work* charlie!

Charlie I *know*!

Toni *You* should try it!

Charlie Okay … go back to sleep … go back to sleep toni.

Toni I will. (*Her head hits the pillow.*)

Charlie Go back to (*shouts*) fucking *sleep*!

Toni raises her head.

It's always the same innit … it's always the fucking same.

Pause.

Toni What?

Charlie Whenever we talk about something.

Toni *Talk* … !?

Charlie Yes *talk* … !

Toni smirks.

You twist things *round*!

Toni Who does?

Charlie *You* do … ! You never stick to the point.

Toni And what is the point?

Charlie sighs.

Charlie We're not talking about if i work.

Toni You don't!

Charlie *I know i don't!*

Pause.

Toni Why don't you work charlie?

Charlie sighs.

Charlie We've been through this ...

Toni Have we?

Charlie Yes ... we have ... (*shouts*) a thousand times!

Toni Well?

Charlie I don't work ... b/cos ... i dunno what to do ... i dunno what to do toni.

Toni Don't you?

Charlie *No.*

Toni That's handy.

Charlie sighs.

How about working ... ? Hmm ... ?

Charlie Doing *what*!?

Toni *Anything*!

Charlie I *told* ya ... ! I don't *wanna* do anything ... i wanna do *something*.

Toni So you do nothing ... great.

Charlie sighs.

Wake up charlie.

Charlie (*shouts*) No *you* wake up! (*He walks up to the futon and pulls back the duvet. Shouts*) Wake up! (*Long pause.*) You think just cos i do nothing ... that means i do nothing.

Toni That's right.

Charlie You think you gotta do something.

Toni That's right.

Charlie Well let me tell ya something toni … just cos you do nothing don't mean you do nothing … and just cos you do something … don't mean you do nothing.

Toni looks bemused.

Toni What?

Charlie I'm just saying … you're still doing nothing if you do something.

Toni smirks.

Toni So that's why you do nothing is it?

Charlie I told ya … i don't do nothing … and even if i did … i'd rather do that than …

Pause.

Toni What?

Charlie What everyone else does.

Toni Everyone else *works*!

Charlie I *know*!

Toni Everyone else *does things*!

Charlie What *things*?

Toni *Things* … charlie … *things* … look around you … *things*!

Charlie Forget about *things* toni … life ain't *about* things!

Toni No?

Charlie *No*!

Toni What is it about?

Charlie (*shouts*) *Life* … ! (*quieter*) It's about life toni.

Toni smirks.

It's about going out … for a day … for a picnic.

Toni smirks.

It's about a picnic. (*Pause.*) You just want me to be a cunt … like all the other cunts.

Pause.

Toni What cunts?

Charlie points outside.

Charlie Out *there*!

Toni Why they cunts charlie?

Charlie (*shouts*) Ask *them*!

Pause.

Toni Everyone's a cunt in your book aren't they?

Charlie No.

Toni Who isn't?

Pause.

Charlie You want me to be like your doctor friend.

Toni looks bemused.

Toni What?

Charlie Your doctor friend.

Toni twigs.

Toni So that's what this is about.

Charlie You want me to be a doctor.

Toni Don't be stupid.

Charlie How's that stupid?

Toni It just is.

Charlie So why dya fuck him?

Toni groans.

(*shouts*) Why dya *fuck* him!?

Pause.

Toni You're always the same.

Charlie Oh so it's *my* fault now is it?

Toni Maybe it is.

Charlie *I* get it. (*Pause.*) *You* fucked him but it's *my* fault.

Toni Ask yourself *why* though charlie.

Charlie *What*?

Toni Ask yourself *why*.

Charlie *Why*!?

Toni *Why* … ! *Why* did i fuck him!

Charlie (*shouts*) B/cos you're a *cunt*!

Pause. Toni starts to cry.

I'm sorry.

Toni You never think of me charlie.

Charlie What? (*Pause.*) That's rich … what have i been doing all day … ? Hey? (*Pause.*) Waiting for you. (*Pause.*) I thought we were going out.

Toni *You* thought.

Charlie Yes *i* thought … we were going on a picnic remember?

Toni No *you* were.

Charlie (*shouts*) *Remember*!?

Toni (*shouts*) I was trying to sleep!

Charlie (*shouts*) Well that makes a change!

Toni (*shouts*) I *work*!

Charlie (*shouts*) I *know* … ! That's all you *do*!

Charlie kicks the desk in anger. Toni flinches. A bottle of wine falls and breaks. Charlie stares at the mess solemnly. He crouches and puts his head in his hands. Long pause.

It's easy for you.

Pause.

Toni What is … ? Why?

Pause.

Charlie It just is.

Toni Why charlie … ? Why's it easy for me?

Charlie You can deal with the cunts … you can talk to em.

Toni What dya mean?

Pause.

Charlie I can't.

Pause.

Toni Why not?

Pause.

Charlie Remember that time ... i picked you up ... from work ... and that bloke with the wig came up to you?

Toni thinks back.

Toni No – what bloke?

Charlie Yes you do ... that old bloke ... he was wearing a wig.

Toni (*to herself*) A wig?

Charlie A toupee ... you know ... he gave you a big bunch of flowers.

Toni Oh yeah.

Charlie Remember?

Pause.

Toni So?

Charlie He said his mum had told him about you.

Toni That's right.

Charlie His old mum ... how you looked after her ... how you talked to her.

Pause.

Toni So?

Charlie She said you were her favourite nurse.

Pause.

Toni So?

Pause.

Charlie So you thanked him and that ... and smiled ... and said it was nothing ... 'nothing'.

44

Toni So?

Pause.

Charlie So i looked at him … and i thought … 'you're wearing a wig you cunt'.

Pause.

Toni What?

Charlie I looked at him tone … straight in the eye … and i thought … 'you're wearing a wig you cunt fuck off'.

Toni He was just being nice.

Charlie I know. (*Pause.*) He had a crease all down his strides. (*He draws an imaginary vertical line.*) 'Straight'.

Toni What's wrong with that?

Charlie Nothing.

Toni Listen charlie.

Charlie looks at Toni inquiringly.

Dya think i like it?

Pause.

Charlie What?

Toni Dya think i like being nice all day … to everyone … ? It's my job!

Charlie chuckles.

What's so funny?

Charlie Daffodils.

Toni What?

Charlie He gave you daffodils. (*He ponders.*) Are daffodils yellow?

Toni nods.

He gave you daffodils.

Toni So?

Charlie What good are daffodils?

Toni They're pretty.

Pause.

Charlie He thinks just cos he gives you daffodils that makes up for it.

Toni For what?

Charlie The wig!

Toni sighs.

That's what he thinks.

Toni Charlie … !

Charlie He's gonna go through life …

Toni *Charlie … !*

Charlie No let me finish.

Toni sighs.

He's gonna go through life giving people daffodils and thinking they won't think he's a cunt.

Toni sighs.

And you know the unbelievable thing? (*Pause.*) Toni.

Toni *What?*

Charlie They *won't*!

Pause.

Toni Charlie i been on my feet all day.

Charlie I know.

Toni I'm tired.

Charlie I *know*!

Toni I need to sleep.

Pause.

Charlie What about me?

Toni What *about* you?

Charlie smirks.

Charlie That says it all dunnit … that says it (*shouts*) fucking *all*!

Toni groans.

Toni Okay. You win. (*She rises.*) Happy?

They stare at each other. Toni puts on her slippers and walks off. She returns holding a damp cloth. She starts mopping up the wine. Charlie watches her.

Charlie What's the matter tone?

Toni *You.*

Charlie What've i done?

Toni Can't you see i'm tired.

Charlie I know. (*Pause.*) Toni. (*Pause.*) Toni.

Toni What?

Charlie You can sleep in the park.

Toni smirks.

Toni Great.

Pause.

Charlie I'll make some coffee.

Toni I don't want coffee.

Charlie But you like coffee.

Toni stops mopping.

Toni (*shouts*) I don't want coffee!

Charlie Alright!

Toni (*shouts*) *Listen* to me!

Charlie (*shouts*) Alright!

Toni continues mopping.

Why can't we talk normally?

Toni stops mopping.

Toni What's 'normally' charlie?

Charlie I mean like normal people.

Toni You mean *cunts*?

Charlie Hey?

Toni Is that what you mean?

Charlie No.

Toni You wanna talk like *cunts*? (*She walks over to the closet.*)

Charlie I never said that.

Toni puts on a pair of tracksuit bottoms.

All i wanted was to have a good time … for once.

Toni Then have a good time.

Charlie *With you* … ! I thought we could go out together … catch the sun … see some friends … we never see each

other toni … i thought today'd be different … look …
(*He points at where the wine was.*) I even bought some …
(*He sees the wine has gone.*) wine. (*He stares at where the
wine was.*)

Toni It's all about you innit.

Charlie What?

Toni It's all about you … *you* wanna go for a picnic …
you wanna go in the sun … *you* wanna see some friends
… well come on then *let's go!* (*She picks up her trainers.*)

Charlie I don't want to.

Toni bursts into laughter.

Toni Look at you.

Charlie What?

Toni You're not even dressed.

Charlie So?

Toni You're not even dressed.

Charlie So?

*Toni throws her trainers at Charlie who cowers. Toni's
voice cracks helplessly.*

Toni You're not even dressed … look at you … you're
not even … (*She falls on her knees and cries.*) dressed.

Charlie looks at Toni tentatively.

Charlie Toni.

Toni (*shouts*) Come on!

Charlie What?

Toni (*shouts*) Let's go!

Charlie (*shouts*) No!

Toni (*shouts*) Why not!?

Charlie (*shouts*) Cos you *spoilt* it! (*Pause.*) You spoilt it toni.

   Toni smirks.

Toni I always spoil it.

Charlie That's right … you do.

Toni So why you with me?

Charlie Good question.

Toni Why you with me charlie?

   Pause.

Charlie That's it.

Toni What?

Charlie This.

   Pause.

Toni What?

Charlie This is the last time toni.

Toni What is?

Charlie *This* is. (*Pause.*) It's not worth it.

Toni So go.

Charlie What?

Toni Go.

Charlie I can't take any more.

Toni So don't. (*Pause.*) Don't charlie. (*Pause.*)

Charlie What dya mean?

Pause.

Toni I mean don't.

Blackout.

SCENE FOUR

NW3. North Star pub. Tuesday. 9.00 p.m. Pints of beer. Charlie and **Davey** *are sitting at a table.*

Davey I split up with emma yesterday.

Charlie You're joking?

Davey Nah.

Charlie How come?

Davey Well remember that spanish girl i told you about?

Charlie Maria.

Davey Monica.

Charlie That's the one.

Davey Well ...

Charlie gapes at Davey.

Charlie You never?

Davey smiles coyly.

You crafty sod.

Davey smiles coyly.

When?

Davey Last week.

Charlie What happened?

Davey Well ... she came to the shop on tuesday.

Charlie Yeah ... ?

Davey No – wednesday.

Charlie Yeah ... ?

Davey And she's with her mate – isabel.

Charlie's eyes light up.

Charlie Isabel?

Davey Yeah.

Charlie Shit.

Davey From 'andalusia'.

Charlie From where?

Davey It's near spain.

Charlie nods.

Charlie Oh.

Davey It's by the mountains.

Charlie What mountains?

Davey The *spanish* mountains.

Charlie nods.

Charlie Oh.

Davey Anyway she comes up to me.

Charlie Yeah ... ?

Davey And asks if i got the smashing pumpkins.

Charlie looks bemused.

Charlie The smashing what?

Davey They're a band.

Charlie Oh yeah.

Davey So i says 'yeah'.

Charlie So?

Davey So i fetch the record.

Pause.

Charlie *And*?

Davey She bought it.

Pause.

Charlie Is that it?

Davey What?

Charlie Is that why you split up with emma!?

Davey No!

Charlie Well *what*!?

Davey Don't ya get it?

Charlie No!

Davey She didn't *wanna* buy the record.

Charlie Didn't she?

Davey No ... ! It was just a decoy.

Charlie A what?

Davey A *ploy* ... to see me like ... dya get me?

Pause.

Charlie Davey.

Davey What?

Charlie Maybe she likes em.

Davey Who?

Charlie The mashed potatoes.

Davey looks bemused.

Davey What?

Charlie Maybe she likes em.

Davey Of *course* she likes em.

Charlie Well then.

Davey She wouldn't *buy* em if she didn't *like* em.

Charlie Exactly.

Davey That's not the point.

Charlie What is?

Davey The point is she coulda bought em *anywhere*. (*He taps his temple with his finger.*) *Capice?*

Pause.

Charlie She lives round the corner.

Davey What?

Charlie She lives round the fucking corner.

Davey So?

Charlie So she's hardly gonna traipse to dulwich for a poxy record now is she? (*Pause.*) Be fair.

Davey I ain't told ya what happened.

Charlie What happened?

Davey That's what i'm coming to.

Charlie Go on then.

Davey sighs.

Davey So she pays for the record ... with her hard earned loot ... course i give her a staff discount ...

Charlie What?

Davey winks at Charlie knowingly.

Davey And she's well chuffed.

Charlie You don't give me a staff discount.

Davey And she says ... check this ...

Charlie What?

Davey Her record player's ... 'broken'.

Charlie gapes at Davey.

Charlie What?

Davey nods smugly.

She says that?

Davey nods smugly.

That's a different story.

Davey smiles smugly.

Why didn't you say?

Davey I was coming to it.

Charlie Shit.

Davey Not only that but her mate ...

Charlie Isabel.

Davey She ain't *got* a record player.

Charlie What?

Davey She's into CDs in't she.

Charlie Is she?

Davey nods.

That's handy.

Davey I know.

They laugh.

So i says 'why ya buying a record then?' and she says ... check this ... she's hoping 'someone' might fix it. (*He winks at Charlie knowingly.*)

Charlie Well that's you buggered innit.

Davey What?

Charlie You couldn't fix a sarnie.

Davey looks at Charlie reproachfully.

Davey See the thing is with these foreign girls ...

Charlie What?

Davey You gotta understand their culture.

Charlie What culture?

Davey Exactly – they ain't got none.

They laugh.

You gotta be ac*custom*ed to their *customs*.

Charlie What customs?

Davey Like in spain say – after lunch – they kip!

Charlie What?

Davey That's it! They don't get up till dinner.

Charlie What?

Davey It's called a 'fiesta'.

Charlie Shit. (*Pause.*) No wonder they're a third world economy.

Davey Exactly!

Charlie With their workforce all asleep.

Davey Exactly! They turn up at ten, have their elevenses, have lunch, and *hit the sack*! That's it! That's their working day … ! Goodnight sienna.

Charlie looks bemused.

Charlie Hey?

Davey Meanwhile the japs are building rockets on the internet.

Charlie Intercom.

Davey *And* that! Where's the competition!?

Charlie Lazy bunch of spic bastards.

Davey I know.

Charlie No wonder there's inflation. (*Pause.*) So … ?

Davey looks at Charlie inquiringly.

What happened with monica?

Davey Maria.

Charlie That's the one.

Davey She asked me out for a drink.

Charlie What?

Davey Yeah.

Charlie Just like that?

Davey They're forward these spanish girls i told ya ... they're 'un-inhibited'.

Charlie 'Un-what'?

Davey Inhibited.

Charlie You mean they're desperate.

Davey No i mean ...

    Charlie laughs mockingly.

They're *freer* that's all.

Charlie Freer?

Davey Yeah!

Charlie Is that what it's called?

Davey It's on account of franco.

Charlie Is it?

Davey Yeah.

Charlie Who's franco?

Davey *General* franco.

Charlie Oh him.

Davey He put the blockers on it.

Charlie Did he?

    Davey nods.

On what?

Davey You know ... (*He raises his eyebrows.*) Rumpty tumpty.

Charlie Did he!?

Davey That's why they all come here.

Charlie Is it?

Davey So they can … (*He raises his eyebrows.*) 'siesta'.

Charlie Hombre!

Davey Arriba!

Charlie My man!

They laugh and slap hands.

So what did monica …

Davey Maria.

Charlie Say.

Davey She said her and her mate …

Charlie Isabel.

Davey Yeah. Were going for a drink … and would i like to … (*He raises his eyebrows.*) 'come'.

Charlie Shit.

Davey So i said …

Charlie 'Yeah'.

Davey Obviously.

Charlie Yeah.

Davey So i locked up.

Charlie There and then?

Davey On the *spot*. I don't mess around charlie.

Charlie Don't ya?

Davey No. When it comes to women i'm like a leopard in the desert.

Charlie A what?

Davey A lion in hawaii.

Charlie A what?

Davey A panther in parsons green.

Charlie looks bemused.

Charlie Say *what*?

Davey You gotta act *quick*. It's no good standing on the shore of time watching everyone sailing.

Charlie What shore?

Davey I'm talking metaphysically.

Charlie nods.

Charlie Oh.

Davey You gotta be out there – *navigating*!

Charlie looks bemused.

Charlie So you locked up … ?

Davey nods.

Davey And we all hit the boozer.

Charlie Safe.

Davey Totally sorted.

Charlie So what happened?

Davey Nothing.

Charlie looks bemused.

All we did was chat.

Charlie Chat?

Davey Yeah ya know – talking.

Charlie Talking?

Davey nods.

That's *it*!?

Davey It weren't ordinary talking though was it.

Charlie Weren't it?

Davey No ... it was like ... i dunno ... like we were long lost friends.

Charlie You what?

Davey Yeah.

Charlie Long lost *what*?

Davey Friends.

Charlie looks bemused.

Charlie What's got into you?

Davey Nothing.

Charlie Listen davey.

Davey What?

Charlie You don't talk to girls.

Davey Don't ya?

Charlie No ... well you do ... if you *have* to ... when there's no *alternative* ... but you gotta remember *why* you're talking to em.

Davey Have ya?

Charlie Yeah.

Davey And why are ya?

Charlie You know.

Davey shakes his head.

You don't get it do ya?

Davey Get what?

Charlie The game.

Davey What game?

Charlie raises his eyebrows.

That's all it is to you innit?

Charlie nods gleefully.

Well i'll tell you something.

Charlie What?

Davey I'm *tired* of games.

Charlie What?

Davey I'm *tired* of second guessing.

Charlie looks bemused.

I'm *tired* of not knowing the score.

Pause.

Charlie You sound tired mate.

Davey I am!

Pause.

Charlie So what's so great about this monica?

Davey Maria.

Charlie That's the fella.

Davey She's different.

Charlie smirks.

She is.

Charlie How?

Davey Well for one thing she's older than your average woman.

Charlie Yeah?

Davey nods.

How old?

Davey Thirty-six.

Charlie gapes at Davey.

Charlie What?

Davey nods smugly.

Shit.

Davey She don't look it she looks about twenty.

Charlie Does she?

Davey And she's got ...

Charlie What?

Davey Spanish 'sensuality'.

Charlie looks bemused.

Charlie Spanish what?

Davey 'Sensuality'.

Charlie Shit.

Davey They're different latin girls.

Charlie Are they? How?

Davey They're more … you know …

Charlie No.

Davey Latin.

Charlie Are they?

Davey They're more … what's the word?

Charlie shrugs.

'Expressive' … they 'express' themselves …

Charlie Do they?

Davey Better.

Pause.

Charlie Shit.

Davey If only she spoke english i'd be laughing.

Charlie What … you mean … ?

Davey shakes his head ruefully.

Davey Not a word … all she knows are beatle songs …
hey fucking jude and all that.

Charlie laughs.

Sergeant bloody pepper.

Charlie So if she can't speak … ?

Davey It ain't that … i don't really care … you know
what it's like when you meet someone new.

Charlie Yeah.

Davey You come outa yourself don't ya.

Charlie Do ya?

Davey Yeah … you say all those things you been wanting

to say … for ages.

Charlie What things?

Davey taps his temple with his finger.

Davey All the crazy stuff … things ya never knew you were thinking … you feel *free*.

Charlie looks bemused.

Charlie So you seeing her again?

Davey Yeah.

Charlie When?

Davey Next week.

Charlie Where?

Davey Dunno … she dunno london … she wants to see the sights.

Charlie ponders.

I thought i'd take her to the arsenal.

Charlie What?

Davey Yeah.

Charlie Don't do that.

Davey She might like it.

Charlie Don't do that.

Davey She *likes* football.

Charlie *Exactly* … ! Take her to a garden centre or something.

Davey looks at Charlie reproachfully.

So did ya tell emma?

Davey About monica?

Charlie Maria.

Davey You're joking ... ! She'd have gone *spare* ... i just made up a yarn.

Charlie And?

Davey She went *spare*.

They laugh.

I had to lock myself in the closet.

Charlie Shit.

Davey It was doing me in though charlie.

Charlie What was?

Davey Emma. I had to leave her.

Charlie Why?

Davey She's changed.

Charlie How?

Davey Guess what she wants to be now?

Charlie What?

Davey A lawyer.

Charlie What?

Davey A fucking lawyer!

Charlie Shit.

Davey She keeps talking about 'test cases'.

Charlie What's that?

Davey shakes his head ruefully.

Davey You don't wanna know.

Pause.

Charlie Shame.

Davey What?

Charlie I like emma.

Davey So do i.

Pause.

Charlie I like emma.

Davey So do i.

Pause.

Charlie She's alright.

Davey I know!

Pause.

Charlie Shame.

Davey Listen charlie.

Charlie What?

Davey Sometimes you have to let things go.

Charlie Do ya?

Davey Have you ever see that film?

Charlie What film?

Davey With de niro.

Charlie ponders.

Charlie Crocodile dundee?

Davey That's the one.

They laugh.

Anyway there's a scene in it where he's tapping his watch cos it's stopped and the fella he's with says 'why ya always tapping your watch?'.

Charlie nods attentively.

And de niro says 'cos it's broken'.

Charlie nods attentively.

So the fella says 'well why dya wear it then?'.

Charlie Exactly.

Davey And de niro says 'cos my missus gave it me'.

Charlie Ahh.

Davey So the fella says 'well where's your missus now?'.

Charlie nods attentively.

And de niro says 'she's shacked up with the fucking neighbour!'.

Pause.

Charlie So?

Davey So every time he checks the time and it says five past four when it's ten to twelve he thinks of his ex and he starts pining.

Pause.

Charlie So?

Davey So the fella says … 'sometimes you gotta throw *away* the old watch … and get a new one'.

Charlie gapes at Davey.

Charlie So what happened?

Davey Well in the end he got him back but he let him go cos his boss was a cunt and …

Charlie I mean with the watch.

Davey Oh the watch.

Charlie Yeah!

Davey He threw it didn't he?

Charlie gapes at Davey.

Charlie Did he?

Davey So how's toni?

Charlie She's alright.

Davey looks at Charlie knowingly.

Guess who i saw yesterday?

Davey Who?

Charlie Ruby 2 shoes.

Davey gapes at Charlie.

Davey Shit.

Charlie Guess what she said to me?

Davey What?

Charlie She said … out of all tone's friends … *i* was her fave.

Davey gapes at Charlie.

Davey What?

Charlie nods smugly.

She never?

Charlie She did.

Davey She was messing.

Charlie She weren't … she said i was never intimidating.

Davey looks bemused.

Davey What?

Charlie And you know what i thought?

Davey What's that?

Charlie I thought … *why* wasn't i?

Davey Hey?

Charlie I mean *why* wasn't i intimidating … ? I'm an intimidating guy.

Davey Sure you are.

Charlie What's so 'un-intimidating' about me?

Davey Nothing. (*Pause.*) So what?

Charlie looks at Davey inquiringly.

What's it matter?

Charlie It don't. (*Pause.*) She wouldn't say that to de niro.

Davey What?

Charlie She wouldn't say that to de niro … she wouldn't go up to de niro and say 'excuse me bobby i'm sorry to trouble ya but you're not very intimidating' would she?

Davey looks bemused.

Davey No.

Charlie Well then.

Davey Why dya wanna be intimidating?

Charlie I don't.

Davey You do.

Charlie I don't ... i just don't wanna be ...

Pause.

Davey What?

Charlie A cunt.

Pause.

Davey Tone still loves her.

Charlie What?

Davey Tone ... he still loves her.

Charlie Who?

Davey Ruby.

Charlie smirks.

Charlie No he don't.

Davey He does.

Charlie Says who?

Davey No-one ... that's not the point ... he's still cut up about her that's all ... who can blame him.

Charlie What?

Davey You know ... ruby ... (*He raises his eyebrows.*) She's alright.

Charlie sneers at Davey.

Charlie What?

Davey raises his eyebrows.

Davey She's got what it takes.

Charlie sneers at Davey.

Charlie Don't talk about her like that.

Davey What?

Charlie Your mate's ex.

Davey So … ? What do you care? (*He twigs.*) Shit you shagged her didn't you?

Charlie What?

Davey You shagged her.

Charlie No i never.

Davey You did … you shagged ruby 2 shoes … *shit*!

Charlie I never!

Davey You did!

   Charlie smiles wryly at Davey.

Holy shit.

   They laugh.

So you gonna tell tone?

Charlie *Tone*!?

Davey Not *tone* … to*ni* … your girlfriend.

Charlie Oh.

   They laugh.

Are you *mad*!?

Davey You'll have to.

Charlie Why?

Davey She'll find out.

Charlie No she won't … you never told emma about you.

Davey That's different.

Charlie How?

Davey It just is … me and emma broke up … there was no *need*.

Charlie Well me and toni *ain't* breaking up.

Davey No?

Charlie No … let me tell ya … me and tone are like … (*He raises his hand and crosses his middle and index fingers firmly.*) *that.*

Davey nods. Pause.

Davey So how was ruby?

Blackout.

Last Part

SCENE ONE

...le's pub. Thursday. 10.00 p.m.
... Spiders from Mars in the back-
grou... ...r. Charlie is sitting at a table. **Kelly**
walks on.

Charlie Oh hi ... kelly ain't it?

Kelly Yeah ... hi.

Charlie It's charlie.

Kelly I know.

They laugh.

Charlie How's it going?

Kelly Fine ... how about you?

Charlie Oh fine ... great ... you're a mate of ... lee's ... ?

Kelly That's right.

Charlie How is he?

Kelly He's fine ... you know lee ... he's ...

Charlie and Kelly 'Pukka'.

Charlie Yeah.

They laugh.

Would you like a drink?

Kelly No thanks i'm fine.

Pause.

Charlie Great. (*Pause.*) So how's it going?

Kelly Okay.

Pause.

Charlie Weren't you at that party in abercorn ... ?

Kelly That's right.

Charlie I thought you were.

Kelly Yeah.

Charlie That was a good party.

Kelly Was it?

Charlie Don't ya reckon?

Kelly I don't remember – i was off my nut.

Charlie Was ya?

Kelly nods.

Yeah.

They laugh.

I thought you looked a bit peaky.

Kelly Peaky?

Charlie Yeah ya know ... 'gone'.

They laugh.

Kelly I was.

Charlie Would you like to sit down?

Kelly Okay. (*She sits down and pulls out her Benson & Hedges.*) Dya want one?

Charlie No thanks i got my own ... i can't smoke those things anyway.

Kelly Why not?

Charlie They're too strong.

Kelly What do you smoke?

Charlie pulls out his Camel Lights and shows them to Kelly.

I can't stand those things.

Charlie They're good for you.

Kelly Are they?

Charlie Yeah … ten a day and you're laughing.

Kelly laughs.

Kelly How can cigarettes be good for you?

Charlie These ones are … besides …

Kelly lights their cigarettes.

They're better than bennies.

Kelly Let's not fight about cigarettes.

Charlie Okay.

They laugh.

What *shall* we fight about?

Kelly Why should we fight about anything?

Charlie I thought that's what men and women do.

Kelly Not always.

Charlie looks startled.

Do you fight a lot then?

Charlie shakes his head.

Charlie Nah not me … i'm a little sweetie.

Kelly looks at Charlie dubiously.

So what shall we fight about?

Kelly laughs.

What beer you drinking?

Kelly Grolsch.

Charlie looks at Kelly approvingly.

Charlie Safe.

Charlie raises his bottle. Kelly raises hers. They clink drinks.

Charlie and Kelly Cheers.

Charlie I knew we had something in common.

Kelly Did you?

Charlie The moment i saw you.

Kelly How come?

Charlie ponders.

Charlie I just knew.

Kelly laughs.

Where you from?

Kelly London.

Charlie Me too!

They laugh.

You see – uncanny.

Kelly Well we are *in* london.

Charlie Double uncanny.

Kelly laughs.

What part of london?

Kelly Highgate.

Charlie Nice.

Kelly How about you?

Charlie Kentish.

Kelly Hmm ...

Charlie and Kelly Not so nice.

Charlie I know.

They laugh.

You dissing my manor?

Kelly No.

Charlie Good.

Kelly Why what would you do about it?

Charlie ponders.

Charlie I might ... never talk to you again.

Kelly That'd be nice.

Charlie Would it?

Kelly nods.

But then we wouldn't be friends.

Kelly We're not.

Charlie I know ... but we might be ... one day you might look back and say that was the day i met charlie.

Kelly I doubt it.

Charlie Why?

Kelly I meet a lot of people.

Charlie Do you?

Kelly nods.

I bet you do.

Kelly Why should i remember you?

Charlie B/cos ... i got odd socks on look. (*He shows Kelly his socks.*)

Kelly Oh yeah.

Charlie See.

They laugh.

Kelly Yeah.

Charlie So you come from highgate?

Kelly Yeah.

Charlie Where dya go to school?

Kelly I went to boarding school.

Charlie Shit ... where was that?

Kelly In the country.

Charlie Shit ... how come?

Kelly My mum sent me there.

Charlie Why?

Kelly What dya mean?

Charlie Didn't she like you?

Kelly Of course she did!

Charlie Well?

Pause.

Kelly If you really wanna know …

Charlie nods.

She was having a hard time.

Charlie I'm sorry.

Kelly That's okay … besides she thought it'd do me good.

Charlie And did it?

Kelly ponders.

Kelly It was okay. (*Pause.*) It was run by nuns.

Charlie What?

Kelly Nuns.

Charlie looks bemused.

Charlie Why?

Kelly It was a convent school.

Charlie Shit. (*He shakes his head.*)

Kelly What's the matter?

Charlie I never knew they did that.

Kelly Did what?

Charlie Did that shit … shit.

Kelly It's normal.

Charlie No it ain't.

Kelly It is.

Charlie It ain't … it ain't normal to have a bunch of nuns telling you what to do.

Kelly They don't.

Charlie Telling you how to do things ... telling you you *gotta* do things ... like doing things is all that *counts*.

Kelly They're not like that.

Charlie They are ... why else would they be nuns?

Kelly Why would anyone be anything?

Charlie Exactly ... ! That's what i tell tone.

Kelly Who's tone?

Pause.

Charlie No-one ... she's just a friend. (*Pause.*) So were there any boys?

Kelly looks at Charlie inquiringly.

At convent school.

Kelly No.

Charlie What did ya do?

Kelly What dya mean?

Charlie I mean for hobbies.

Kelly I studied!

Charlie Shit. (*Pause.*) And?

Kelly looks at Charlie inquiringly.

Did ya go to college?

Kelly Yeah.

Charlie Where?

Kelly Manchester.

Charlie nods.

Charlie What did you do?

Kelly Made up for lost time.

Charlie No i mean …

They laugh.

What subject?

Kelly English.

Charlie nods.

Charlie You know that's always puzzled me.

Kelly What has?

Charlie I mean how you can study english in england.

Kelly What?

Charlie I mean it seems like a strange place to study it.

Kelly Why?

Charlie I dunno … i'd have thought you'd have to go *abroad* to study it.

Kelly Why?

Charlie It just seems a bit strange … that's all … like studying religion in china.

Kelly What?

Charlie Yeah … or war in yugoslavia … it's a bit … close to home … don't ya reckon?

Kelly No.

Charlie looks surprised.

Charlie What?

Kelly It's good to look close to home.

Charlie Why?

Kelly So you know what's going on indoors.

Charlie looks bemused.

Charlie Why dya wanna know that?

Kelly So you can look *outside* better.

Charlie looks bemused.

Charlie Why dya wanna do that?

Kelly In case you're missing something.

Pause.

Charlie Shit.

Kelly So did *you* go to college?

Charlie shakes his head.

Charlie Nah.

Kelly Why not?

Charlie ponders.

Charlie I dunno … i looked at all the subjects and … i couldn't be fucked.

Kelly Why not?

Charlie I just said.

Kelly No you never.

Charlie I did … i wanted to go … i thought about it … i woulda had to leave home … i had a girlfriend.

Kelly Tone?

Charlie nods.

Charlie Yeah.

Kelly So … ?

Charlie shrugs.

Did she go to college?

Charlie nods.

Charlie Nursing school.

Kelly Well?

Charlie ponders.

Charlie It didn't fit in with my plans.

Kelly What were they?

Charlie thinks back.

Charlie I can't remember.

Pause.

Kelly So what dya do now?

Charlie This and that.

Kelly What?

Charlie Nothing.

Kelly laughs.

I'm trying to find my niche.

Kelly Are you?

Charlie I know it's out there.

Kelly What are your interests?

Charlie Interests?

Kelly Hobbies.

Charlie Hobbies?

Kelly You know what hobbies are?

Charlie looks at Kelly reproachfully.

Charlie I'm not thick.

Kelly So why dya act it?

Charlie I don't act anything.

Kelly looks at Charlie dubiously.

You think you know me.

Kelly I know your type.

Charlie How?

Kelly You remind me of someone.

Charlie Who?

Kelly My ex-boyfriend.

Charlie raises his eyebrows.

Charlie He a sweetie too is he?

Kelly No he's a layabout.

Pause.

Charlie I ain't a layabout i told you.

Kelly What are you?

Charlie I'm a person … look at me … i'm a real life fucking person … i got gifts.

Kelly What gifts?

Charlie ponders.

Charlie Lots of em.

Kelly Well then.

Charlie What?

Kelly You got lots to choose from.

Charlie I know ... that's the trouble ... i gotta narrow it down ... i'm thinking of working in television.

Kelly Are you?

Charlie Yeah.

Kelly As what?

Charlie As a junior presenter or something.

Kelly What's that?

Charlie Well ... basically ... you present stuff right ... but you're only a junior.

Kelly So what does that mean?

Charlie It means ... (*Charlie ponders.*) Fuck knows what it means.

They laugh.

So what do *you* do?

Kelly I'm a production manager.

Charlie Are you?

Kelly nods.

What's that?

Kelly I'm in charge of everything.

Charlie looks impressed.

Charlie Like what?

Kelly Like everything on the shoot.

Charlie What shoot?

Kelly The *film* shoot.

Charlie I get it ... and how many of them dya do?

Kelly What?

Charlie I mean at a time.

Kelly Just the one.

Charlie Why's that?

Kelly B/cos that's all you *can* do.

Charlie Right ... so how dya get into that?

Kelly I just kept applying.

Charlie How?

Kelly Through ads.

Charlie What ads?

Kelly In the guardian.

Pause.

Charlie So where dya buy the guardian?

Kelly What?

Charlie I'm just curious.

Kelly looks bemused.

Kelly Why?

Charlie No reason.

Pause.

Kelly I have it delivered.

Charlie It's good that.

Kelly What?

Charlie Having things delivered … it means you don't have to get it yourself … it just turns up … on your doorstep … like magic. (*He smiles.*) Safe.

Kelly Listen charlie i gotta go.

Charlie Don't go.

Kelly I gotta.

Charlie I wanna ask you about your job.

Kelly What about it?

Charlie Dya like it?

Kelly shrugs.

Kelly It's alright.

Charlie But what?

Kelly But nothing. (*Pause.*) It's just not …

Pause.

Charlie What?

Pause.

Kelly What i had in mind.

Charlie Ain't it?

Kelly shakes her head.

What is?

Kelly I dunno.

Charlie But you like it?

Kelly Not really.

Charlie So why dya do it?

Kelly I dunno ... well no i *do* know i suppose.

Charlie What?

Kelly It's fulfilling.

Charlie Is it?

Kelly ponders.

Kelly Nah not really.

They laugh.

That's what you're meant to say innit.

Charlie Is it?

Kelly nods.

I wouldn't know ... i've never had a job.

Kelly Haven't you?

Charlie No ... well that's not true ... i was a barman once.

Kelly That's a job.

Charlie I know ... it didn't work.

Kelly Why not?

Charlie People used to come in and buy drinks ... and i had to give em them ... it was a nightmare.

Kelly checks her watch.

Kelly Listen i gotta go.

Charlie What?

Kelly I'm meeting people.

Charlie Who?

Kelly Friends. (*Pause.*) I'll see ya. (*She gets up.*)

Charlie Don't go.

Kelly What?

Charlie Stay.

Pause.

Kelly I can't.

Charlie I wanna tell you something.

Kelly What?

Pause.

Charlie Sit down.

Kelly What is it?

Pause.

Charlie Everything.

Kelly Like what?

Kelly sits down.

What?

Charlie I wish i'd done what *i'd* wanted to.

Kelly What was that?

Charlie ponders.

Charlie I wanted to be an olympic diver.

Kelly Did you?

Charlie Yeah but i can't swim ... story of my fucking life.

Kelly Why an olympic diver?

Charlie I dunno ... i just used to see em on the telly ... i thought ... you could dive off the top board ... the top fucking board ... eight hundred feet in the air ... and pretend you were diving off the world … just think 'fuck it i'm diving off see ya later' … but you knew the water was there so you were safe … that's what i thought.

Kelly You got some funny ideas.

Charlie I know.

Kelly I wanted to be an actress.

Charlie Really?

Kelly nods.

You still can.

Kelly I can't.

Charlie Why not?

Kelly I'm not beautiful enough.

Charlie You are!

Kelly chuckles coyly.

I mean of course you are.

Kelly I don't have enough confidence.

Charlie You do … ! You got bags full. (*He taps his temple with his finger.*) Confidence is a state of mind.

Kelly Is it?

Charlie It's an optical illusion.

Kelly Is it?

Charlie It's a trick of light … don't be fooled.

Kelly I won't.

Charlie Good.

They laugh.

Kelly You gotta be pretty thick-skinned though.

Charlie Have you?

Kelly nods.

Why?

Kelly To cope with the rejection.

Charlie What rejection?

Kelly Of not getting parts.

Charlie What parts?

Kelly The parts you wanna play.

Pause.

Charlie So don't play any.

Kelly looks bemused.

Kelly So … ?

Charlie looks at Kelly inquiringly.

Are you meeting someone?

Charlie Here?

Kelly Yeah.

Charlie Nah … i'm by myself … i fancied a quiet pint.

Kelly Why?

Charlie I needed to get away.

Kelly From what?

Charlie ponders.

Charlie From the whole thing.

Kelly I know that feeling.

Charlie Do you?

Kelly I think everyone does.

Charlie Do they?

Kelly Well if they don't they should.

Charlie Dya reckon?

Kelly nods.

Sometimes i think it's just me.

Kelly What?

Charlie Who looks at the world … (*He looks around the pub.*) and thinks 'bollocks'.

Kelly chuckles.

What's so funny?

Kelly I'm sorry.

Charlie What?

Kelly You.

Charlie What about me?

Kelly Nothing. (*Pause.*) You make me laugh.

Charlie Why?

Kelly You just do.

Charlie looks bemused.

Anyway carry on.

Charlie No.

Kelly Go on.

Charlie I can't remember where i was.

Kelly You were talking about the world.

Charlie Was i?

Kelly nods.

Oh yeah … i was saying how much i liked it.

Kelly No you weren't.

Charlie I was.

Kelly You were saying something else.

Charlie Well i changed my mind.

Kelly Why?

Charlie Something made me.

Kelly What?

Charlie Something i'm looking at.

Pause.

Kelly I see.

Charlie Do you?

Kelly I think so. (*Pause.*) You're pretty forward aren't you?

Charlie Am i?

Kelly *I'd* say so.

Charlie ponders.

Charlie Yeah … i suppose i am … well spotted.

Kelly laughs.

But let's face it.

Kelly What?

Charlie We're made for each other.

Kelly No we're not!

Charlie We are ... ! We got so much in common.

Kelly We don't!

Charlie We do ... ! We both come from london ... we're both *in* london ... we both drink grolsch ... we both went to boarding school.

Kelly You didn't.

Charlie Yeah but *you* did ... we can't have everything in common that's being unreasonable ... let's see ... we both work in media.

Kelly *You* don't.

Charlie But i will.

Kelly Listen charlie it was nice to meet you.

Charlie And you.

Kelly pecks Charlie on the cheek.

Kelly I think you should get away.

Charlie What?

Kelly Get outa here ... clear your head.

Charlie Where?

Kelly That's up to you.

Charlie Where would *you* go?

Kelly *I'd* go to wales.

Charlie Wales!?

Kelly nods.

That's a bit extreme.

Kelly My mum's got a cottage there.

Charlie Has she?

Kelly nods.

Kelly It's lovely.

Charlie Is it?

Kelly So peaceful … i'm going this weekend.

Charlie With who?

Kelly Lee.

Charlie looks disappointed.

And amy.

Charlie Who's she?

Kelly His girlfriend.

Charlie's eyes light up.

Charlie Just the three of you?

Kelly Yeah.

Charlie Can i come?

Kelly What?

Charlie Go on.

Kelly laughs.

Kelly I dunno.

Charlie I won't be any trouble.

Pause.

Kelly I'll think about it.

Charlie smiles.
Blackout.

SCENE TWO

Wales. Brecon Beacons. Saturday. 6.00 p.m. Flexifoil kite.
Lee is standing with his hands through the straps, holding
the strings. Kelly is sitting on a mound beside him holding
an SLR camera. Charlie is off-stage.

Lee (*shouts*) Hold it above your head ... no above ...
that's it ... now check it's the right way round.

Charlie (*shouts*) How?

Lee (*shouts*) The writing should be facing me ... so i can
read it ... is it?

Charlie (*shouts*) Dunno.

Lee (*shouts*) Then check!

Pause.

Charlie (*shouts*) Okay.

Lee (*shouts*) Now hold it above your head ... that's it ...
now don't hold onto it ... when i say 'go' let go. (*He gets*
the signal. Shouts) Go!

The kite takes flight. Lee tugs at the strings.

Kelly Wow.

Lee I told ya.

Kelly That's brilliant.

Lee It's a bit windy today. (*He does a loop.*)

Kelly Wow look at that ... how dya do that?

Lee I'll show ya.

Kelly Do that again. (*She looks through the camera.*) Wait till i'm focused ... okay.

Lee does a loop. Kelly shoots.

Wow.

Lee Dya get it?

Kelly I think so.

Charlie walks on.

Lee (*to Charlie*) See it?

Charlie Yeah.

Lee Pukka.

Charlie Safe.

Lee It's a good wind today ... pukka ... watch this.

Lee does a double loop.

Kelly Wow!

Lee (*to Charlie*) See that?

Charlie Safe.

Kelly How dya do that?

Lee Come here.

Kelly stands and gives Charlie the camera.

Put your arms around me.

Kelly stands behind Lee and grips his arms.

Now hold my hands.

Kelly grips Lee's hands.

Now feel what i do.

Kelly Okay.

Lee When you wanna go left you pull left. (*He pulls left.*)
See?

Kelly Yeah.

Lee And when you wanna go right ... (*He pulls right.*)
you pull right.

Kelly Wow.

Lee Easy innit?

Kelly So how dya do a loop?

Lee You do the same thing ... you just pull harder ... like
that. (*He does a loop.*)

Kelly Wow!

Lee You see.

Kelly Yeah.

Lee You have to remember to always compensate.

Kelly What dya mean?

Lee Well when you pull one way pull to the other ... like
that. (*He demonstrates.*) Otherwise it falls.

Kelly I get it.

Lee Don't pull too hard or it falls the other way ... like
that. (*He demonstrates.*)

Kelly Right.

Lee You with me?

Kelly Yeah.

Lee Dya wanna go?

Kelly (*to Charlie*) Charlie?

Charlie You go.

Kelly I wanna take pictures. (*She lets go of Lee and takes the camera.*)

Lee (*to Charlie*) Just hold my hands a tick.

Charlie No i'm alright.

Kelly Go on.

Charlie No … i'm alright.

Kelly Go on.

Charlie reluctantly stands behind Lee and grips his hands.

Lee So if ya wanna go left you pull left. (*He pulls left.*)

Charlie Right.

Lee And vice versa. (*He pulls right.*) Okay?

Charlie Yeah.

Lee passes Charlie the straps.

Lee Put your hands in these. (*He lets go of the strings. The kite dips.*)

Charlie Whoah!

Lee tugs at Charlie's arm and the kite rises.

Shit.

Kelly laughs.

Lee Remember what i said – you gotta compensate.

Charlie Right.

Kelly laughs.

Lee Got it?

Charlie I think so.

Lee Okay.

The kite flies safely.

That's it.

Charlie smiles.

Easy.

Charlie Sorted.

Lee Totally pukka.

Kelly You look like such a prat.

Charlie What?

Kelly looks through the camera.

Get off!

Kelly shoots.

Fuck off!

Kelly and Lee laugh.

Kelly And again. (*She shoots.*)

Charlie Get off!

Kelly What's the matter?

Charlie Take some of him.

Lee (*to Kelly*) Go on. (*He poses.*)

Kelly Okay. (*She looks through the camera.*) Smile.

Lee makes a funny face. Kelly shoots. They both laugh.

Wow look at that view.

Kelly points. Lee turns.

Lee Pukka.

Kelly I'm going there … see ya later. (*She runs off.*)

Charlie Where's she gone?

Lee To take pictures.

Charlie shakes his head.

Charlie What is it with her?

Lee What dya mean?

Charlie shrugs.

Charlie There's postcards in town.

Lee So?

Charlie shrugs.

She likes it.

Charlie That's the thing with girls.

Lee What?

Charlie They can't let go … they always gotta be taking snaps … they don't wanna *live* in case they learn something!

Lee That's not true.

Charlie It is … ! They're too *scared* to buy a new watch.

Lee What?

Charlie A new watch … you know … like that film.

Lee What film?

Charlie With de niro … never mind.

Lee looks bemused.

Lee Here let me try.

Charlie passes Lee the straps. Lee flies the kite.

But i thought you and kelly were …

Pause.

Charlie What?

Lee You know.

Charlie Nah … it's not like that.

Lee Why not?

Charlie She won't have it.

They laugh.

Lee Shame.

Charlie I don't care.

Lee Why not?

Charlie B/cos i can't get involved.

Lee Why not?

Charlie B/cos i just split up with someone.

Lee Who?

Charlie Toni.

Lee She your girlfriend?

Charlie shakes his head ruefully.

Charlie Nah.

Lee She the one with short hair?

Charlie Yeah.

Lee Yeah you two are always together.

Pause.

Charlie Not any more.

Lee glances at Charlie.

Lee You missing her?

Charlie chuckles ruefully.

Charlie Just a bit.

Lee I know what it's like.

Charlie Do you?

Lee Yeah. I split up with jane a year ago … you don't get over it.

Charlie Cheers.

Lee I'd been seeing her for six years.

Charlie What?

Lee Six fucking years.

Charlie Shit.

Lee shakes his head ruefully.

Lee So why dya split up?

Charlie She wanted new things.

Lee They always want new things.

Charlie Do they?

Lee nods.

Lee They can't see the old things is better.

Pause.

Charlie Maybe she'll come back.

Lee shakes his head ruefully.

Lee Nah … i thought she might … not now.

Charlie Why?

Lee She's got a new fella.

Charlie Has she?

Lee Yeah. She loves him and everything.

Charlie Does she?

Lee nods.

How dya know?

Lee I seen em together.

Charlie Shit.

Lee Thing is he's a nice bloke.

Charlie Is he?

Lee He used to be my boss.

Charlie What?

Lee I *introduced* them!

Charlie Shit!

Lee What a cunt hey. (*He shakes his head ruefully.*)

Charlie But you said he was a nice … ?

Lee He is … that's the trouble.

Charlie Is he rich?

Lee nods.

Lee Loaded … he's a record producer.

Charlie Shit.

Lee He's got his own studio and everything.

Charlie Shit ... how old is he?

Lee Twenty-nine.

Charlie Shit.

Lee He's almost *thirty*!

Pause.

Charlie Shit.

Lee He ain't got no hair.

Charlie What?

Lee He's bald.

Charlie Is he?

Lee Yeah.

They laugh smugly.

Serves him right.

Charlie Bald bastard.

Lee I know ... how can she go out with someone who's thirty?

Charlie He's probably a father figure.

Lee glances at Charlie.

Lee What?

Charlie All these producers are ... and executives.

Lee Are they?

Charlie Trust me.

Lee But jane's dad's alright.

106

Charlie But is he a producer?

Lee No.

Charlie See … producers bring out the daughterly instincts.

Lee Do they?

Charlie nods knowingly.

Charlie Watch out for doctors an'all.

Lee looks bemused.

Lee Doctors? (*He glances at Charlie.*)

Charlie So what about amy?

Lee She's just a fling.

They laugh.

I like her don't get me wrong … i just can't get over jane.

Charlie Shit.

Lee I can't stop thinking about her … i try not to but i keep bumping into her.

Charlie Do ya?

Lee Yeah.

Charlie Where?

Lee Everywhere.

Charlie How come?

Lee B/cos we got the same friends.

Charlie nods.

Like take last saturday for instance.

Charlie What happened?

Lee I went to a wedding.

Charlie Right.

Lee My *best* mate ... and who should be there?

Charlie Who?

Lee Jane ... the bride was *her* best mate!

Charlie Shit.

Lee I cried.

Charlie What?

Lee I cried.

Charlie When?

Lee At the reception ... i cried.

Charlie gapes at Lee.

Charlie You're joking?

Lee shakes his head.

Lee I was tanked up with booze ... but i still cried.

Charlie Yeah but you were tanked up with booze.

Lee I know.

Charlie It don't count ... it was your mate's wedding ... you're meant to cry.

Lee I made a prat of myself.

Charlie Why?

Lee I poured my heart out to her.

Charlie Shit.

Lee Told her how much i loved her. (*He shakes his head ruefully.*) Big mistake ... said it shoulda been *us* getting wed not them!

Charlie What did she say?

Lee She cried … it was like the rainy season … i told her about amy.

Charlie And?

Lee You know what she said?

Charlie What?

Lee Guess.

Charlie shrugs.

She said she was pleased for me.

Charlie Shit.

Lee Silly bitch … she said she was *pleased* for me … can you believe it … ? She thought no-one'd have me … ! *Me*!? (*He glances at Charlie.*) I mean that's a fucking joke innit.

Charlie So what dya do?

Lee What dya think i did?

They clock each other.

Charlie/Lee You cried./I cried.

Pause.

Charlie See that's different to toni.

Lee Why?

Charlie She'd want me to be miserable.

Lee glances at Charlie.

Lee Looks like she's getting her wish. (*Pause.*) She's on holiday.

Charlie Who is?

Lee Jane … she's gone to mexico … with 'roger'.

Charlie Roger?

Lee Yeah.

Charlie That's his name?

Lee nods.

Shit.

They laugh smugly.

Lee He's called roger he's bald and he's fifty. (*Pause.*) And he's taken her to mexico.

Pause.

Charlie Cunt.

Lee They're gonna have kids.

Charlie Are they?

Lee Yeah.

Charlie How dya know?

Lee It's obvious.

Charlie Is it?

Lee nods.

How long they been going out?

Lee Two weeks.

Charlie smirks.

What?

Charlie That's nothing!

Lee So … ? I can sense it.

Charlie smirks.

Charlie No you can't.

Lee I can.

Charlie How can you? (*Pause.*) You know what *i* reckon?

Lee looks at Charlie inquiringly.

I reckon *you* want kids.

Lee What?

Charlie I reckon *you* want em.

Lee smirks.

That's why you *talk* about em so much!

Lee Fuck off!

Charlie It's true … ! They don't want kids … they're sunning it up in mexico … lovely … why would they want kids?

Lee What would *you* know?

Charlie You're the one who's old.

Lee What?

Charlie Not roger … all this shit about weddings.

Lee So?

Charlie Who *cares*!?

Lee glances at Charlie.

Lee What's got into you?

Charlie How old are you?

Lee Older than you.

Charlie That's for sure … look at you with your fucking kite.

Lee What about it!?

Charlie smirks.

You think you're 'it' don't you?

Charlie What?

Lee You think you're 'it'.

Charlie ponders.

Charlie No.

Lee Yes you do … you think you're everyone's 'honey'.

Charlie ponders.

Charlie No i don't.

Lee Everyone's 'sweetheart' that's you.

Charlie No it ain't.

Lee Look at you … mister 'big'. (*He looks at Charlie scornfully.*) You think you're in the fucking movies.

Lee chuckles mockingly. Charlie glares at Lee. Lee looks up at the kite and becomes absorbed in it so that he only half-listens to Charlie from now on. Pause.

Charlie She's a nurse.

Pause.

Lee Who is?

Charlie Toni.

Pause.

Lee Is she?

Charlie nods.

Charlie One of the best ... people give her flowers.

Lee Do they? What kind?

Charlie Daffodils.

Lee nods.

Complete strangers ... they don't have to ... they do it cos they want to ... can you believe that?

Lee What?

Charlie Giving someone flowers cos you want to?

Lee ponders.

Lee Nah.

Charlie Nor can i. (*Pause.*) She's the only girl i know ... who don't work in television.

Lee What?

Charlie Not only that ... she don't *wanna* work in it ... she *watches* it ... i thought that's what people do ... i thought they *watched* it i never knew they *worked* in it!

Lee Someone has to.

Charlie Yeah but no-one you meet ... ! I mean if everyone works in it who watches it?

Lee ponders.

Lee Me.

Charlie They don't see ... you *have* to watch it ... to know what it's like.

Lee What?

Charlie *Life*!

Pause.

Lee I know what life's like.

Charlie If you don't watch it you're fucked.

Lee Why?

Charlie Cos you dunno what it's like ... to put your feet up ... crack open a can ... and find there's nothing but *bollocks* on.

Pause.

Lee It's getting cold.

Charlie She don't wanna be a newsreader.

Lee What?

Charlie Or an actress ... she just wants to be a nurse.

Lee glances at Charlie.

Lee Are you cold?

Charlie Who you gonna call when you have a heart attack?

Lee Hey?

Charlie When your brain *fucks* up and you can't *talk* ... ! Who you gonna call?

Lee looks bemused.

Lee What?

Charlie You gonna call a newsreader?

Lee No!

Charlie *No* ... ! You're gonna call a *nurse* ... ! What good's a *fucking* newsreader ... !? When you're dying of aids on your deathbed.

Lee What?

Charlie You gonna wanna watch the news? (*He smirks.*) I don't think so.

Lee glances at Charlie.

Lee What's got into you?

Charlie Where do nurses go drinking?

Lee What?

Charlie What pubs?

Lee Why?

Charlie I wanna know.

Pause.

Lee What for?

Pause.

Charlie I lost her.

Pause.

Lee What?

Charlie I lost her.

Charlie looks at his palm.

I had her in my fucking hand and i lost her.

Lee She'll come back.

Charlie shakes his head ruefully.

Charlie She loved me ... she was the best thing i ever had ... and she loved me.

Lee What's the time?

Pause. Charlie looks at his watch.

Charlie Five past … (*He looks again.*) No. (*He taps his watch and puts it to his ear.*) Fucking thing.

Lee glances at Charlie.

Lee You wanna get a new one.

Charlie What?

Lee Spoil yourself.

Charlie Nah.

Lee If it's bust.

Charlie It ain't. (*He winds his watch and it starts ticking.*) It's fine. (*He puts it to his ear.*) See. (*He proudly shows Lee his watch.*)

Lee I'll get kelly. (*He passes Charlie the straps.*) Take these.

Lee walks off. Charlie flies the kite. He tugs too hard and it falls.

Charlie Shit.

Charlie drops the straps and walks off. He walks on holding the kite and the strings which he has tangled into a mess. He picks up the remainder of the strings and stares solemnly at the mess in his hands. Lee and Kelly walk on.

Kelly Hi.

Charlie looks up. Lee sees the mess.

Lee What's that?

Charlie What?

They all look at the mess.

Kelly Shit.

Lee What've you done?

Charlie Nothing.

Lee You fool!

Kelly laughs.

Charlie The kite fell.

Lee So?

Charlie I picked it up.

Lee sighs.

Lee You shoulda left it. (*He takes the string.*) What got into you?

Charlie I thought i was doing you a favour.

Lee A favour?

Kelly laughs.

Shit.

Kelly Come on we'll undo it.

Lee holds out the string.

Lee Look at it. (*He lets the string fall.*)

Kelly Come on. (*She sits down on the mound. She takes a strand of string and starts untangling.*) It'll only take a minute.

Lee chuckles ruefully. He picks up the string.

Lee (*to Charlie*) Take this.

*Charlie takes a strand of string. Lee takes the large weave. They start untangling. A **Man** in his early thirties walks on. He has a broad Welsh accent.*

Man Got it tangled did you?

Charlie looks at the Man scornfully.

Charlie Nah.

The Man laughs.

Man Oh i've done that before … when i was a kid mind.

Kelly laughs.

Been flying your kite then?

Kelly Yeah.

Lee points at Charlie.

Lee Till this prat did this.

The Man laughs. Charlie and Lee glare at each other then continue untangling.

Man Well it's a nice day for it anyway.

Kelly It's lovely.

Man Bit nippy now though … where you from?

Kelly London.

Man London are you?

Kelly nods.

That's nice … here for the weekend?

Kelly That's right.

Man I've been to london.

Kelly Have you?

Charlie drops his hands and stares at the Man scornfully. He keeps this pose until near the end of the scene.

Man Took the kids.

Kelly Ahh.

Man Saw the tower.

Kelly Did you?

Man St. paul's ... the kids loved it.

Kelly I bet they did.

Man Bit pricey though.

Kelly London?

Man Aye.

Kelly I know.

Man The kids wanted an ice cream ... one of them wanted a flake 99 and the other one ... a lobster or something.

Kelly Oyster.

Man That's it. Three pounds!

Kelly What!?

Man Three pounds ... ! I thought blimey you could get a real lobster for that.

Kelly laughs.

Kelly Two kids is it?

Man Aye ... both girls ... sarah's five and louise is two.

Kelly Ahh.

Man Little treasures they are.

Kelly Where are they now?

Man With their mum ... at home ... making dinner i hope.

Kelly laughs. The Man looks at the kite.

They're good little kites those.

Lee Yeah.

Man They're fun things.

Lee Pukka.

Man I'm sorry?

Kelly laughs.

Lee They're … pukka … you know … 'safe'.

Man Safe are they … ? Oh aye … they are that … you can't do any harm with those.

Lee looks bemused.

I bought one for the kiddies.

Lee The kiddies?

Man Aye.

Lee sneers at the Man.

Lee This cost me sixty quid!

The Man gapes at Lee

Man Did it … !? Cor blimey. (*He laughs.*) They musta seen you coming … hey? (*He shakes his head in wonder.*) Sixty quid … cor blimey.

Lee sneers at the Man then continues untangling.

(*to Kelly*) I prefer hang gliding myself.

Kelly Do you?

Man Aye … been doing it … let's see … nearly ten years now.

Kelly Wow … is it dangerous?

Man Oh aye … very … i nearly died once.

Kelly Did you?

Man Aye ... just here it was.

Kelly Where?

The Man points.

Man Top of that hill there see.

Kelly looks at the hill.

Kelly Christ ... what happened?

Man Well the wind dropped see so i had no control so i tried to come in but my leg bent back just as i was landing.

Kelly Shit.

Man And i keeled over.

Kelly Shit.

Man Aye ... it was bad ... luckily i got rescued ... otherwise i'd have died.

Kelly Shit.

Man Aye ... broke my leg ... cracked some ribs ... dislocated my elbow. (*He runs his hand down his back.*) Tore this side of my back.

Kelly Shit.

Man I was in hospital six weeks ... six weeks i was ... doc said it was a 'miracle' i survived.

Kelly Christ.

Man But i still do it.

Kelly Do you?

Man Aye ... oh aye ... love it see ... nothing can stop me.

Kelly It must be a great feeling.

Man It is … aye. (*He looks up at the sky*.) When you're up there. (*He takes a deep breath*.) Nothing like it. (*He looks at Charlie who is still staring at him scornfully. The man smiles*.) Got the time have you?

Pause.

Charlie No.

Man Yes you do … you got it there on your wrist look.

Pause.

Charlie No.

The Man nods.

Man Oh … broken is it … ? You should get a new one.

Charlie stares at the Man scornfully. The Man looks at Kelly and smiles.

Well look i must be off.

Kelly Okay.

Man It was nice to meet you.

Kelly And you.

Man Take care of yourselves … bye.

Kelly Bye.

The Man walks off. Charlie follows him with his eyes. Kelly continues untangling.

He was a nice bloke.

Charlie turns his stare to Kelly.
Blackout.

SCENE THREE

NW5. Toni's bedroom. Tuesday. 7.00 p.m. Primal Scream in the background. The futon is as a sofa. Toni is preparing to go out. The front door shuts in the background.

Toni Hello. (*Pause.*) Hello.

Toni walks tentatively towards the bedroom door. It opens and Charlie appears.

Charlie.

Charlie Hi.

Toni What are you doing?

Charlie What dya mean?

Toni I mean what are you doing here? (*Pause.*) You gave me a shock.

Charlie Did i?

Toni Yes.

Charlie Why?

Toni Why dya think?

Charlie shrugs.

I didn't know who it was.

Charlie Well who else could it be?

Toni I dunno.

Charlie Well then.

Toni You shoulda rung.

Charlie nods.

Charlie So i gotta ring now have i?

Toni Yes … you have.

Charlie I get it.

Toni It's *my* flat charlie.

Charlie I know … i know whose flat it is … here. (*He holds out a pair of keys.*) I came to give you these.

   Pause.

Toni It's alright.

Charlie What?

Toni You can keep em.

Charlie Why?

   Toni shrugs.

Toni Whatever.

Charlie I don't want em. (*Pause.*) Take em.

   Toni sighs.

Toni Okay. (*She takes the keys.*)

Charlie So that's it is it?

Toni What?

Charlie That's it.

Toni What dya mean?

Charlie I mean that's it.

   Pause.

Toni I didn't *ask* for the keys charlie.

Charlie So that's it.

Toni You *gave* them to me.

Pause.

Charlie See ya later. (*He starts to turn.*)

Toni Where you going?

Charlie What do you care?

Toni Of course i care.

Charlie smirks.

You know i do.

Charlie So why you acting like this?

Toni Like what?

Charlie Like *this* … ! Like you don't know me.

Toni I'm not.

Charlie You are … ! Look at you toni … look at you.

Toni What?

Charlie You've changed!

Toni So … ? Maybe i have.

Charlie You have!

Toni Maybe i had to!

Charlie looks bemused.

Charlie Hey?

Toni Something had to.

Charlie Why?

Toni You *know* why.

Charlie shakes his head.

B/cos we're going nowhere.

Pause.

Charlie Yeah but we're going nowhere together.

They chuckle.

See.

Toni What?

Charlie I can still make you laugh.

Toni Of course you can ... you know you can ... maybe that's the trouble.

Charlie looks bemused.

Charlie What?

Toni Maybe it's too easy for you ... maybe i make it too easy.

Charlie To what?

Toni To laugh ... i'm sick of laughing.

Charlie Why?

Toni B/cos it's not a joke anymore.

Charlie I know.

Toni Do you?

Charlie Yes ... i do ... i don't want you to laugh toni ... i just want you to ...

Pause.

Toni What?

Charlie Love me.

Toni I *do* love you.

Charlie But like before.

Toni shakes her head.

Toni I can't.

Charlie Why not?

Toni I just can't ... too many things have happened.

Charlie What's happened? (*Pause.*) Hey? (*Pause.*) Nothing's happened.

Toni Exactly.

Charlie looks bemused.

That's the point.

Charlie Well what dya wanna happen? (*Pause.*) Why's something always gotta happen? (*Pause.*) Why can't things stay the same? (*Pause.*) Everyone wants something to happen but when it does they don't know what to fucking do about it!

Toni looks bemused.

Toni Hey? (*Pause.*) That doesn't make sense.

Charlie That's another thing.

Toni What is?

Charlie Making sense ... i mean everyone wants everyone to make sense but when they do no-one's got a clue what they're on about!

Toni looks bemused.

Toni What?

Charlie Exactly! (*Pause.*) Toni.

Pause.

Toni What?

Charlie I just wish …

Pause.

Toni What?

Charlie I just wish …

Pause.

Toni What?

Charlie I just fucking wish that's all.

Toni *What* do you wish!

Charlie I wish we could be together!

Pause.

Toni Why?

Charlie Why dya think? (*Pause.*) B/cos i love you.

Toni raises her eyebrows.

Toni Do you? (*Pause.*) I'm not sure you do.

Charlie I do.

Toni I'm not sure you can.

Charlie I can. (*Pause.*) I cancan.

Toni chuckles.

I'm a canny lad tone i told ya … i can do anything.

Toni Can you change?

Charlie Easy. (*He opens his arms.*) Tell me what to change and i'll change it.

Toni I'm serious charlie.

Charlie So am i.

Toni I wanna know what happened.

Charlie What dya mean?

Toni What went wrong.

Charlie Nothing.

Toni It *did* … ! When you gonna open your eyes … ? When you gonna start looking at *us* for once instead of looking at people?

Charlie What people?

Toni People … ! You're always slating people … ! People who've nothing to *do* with you … people who don't give two *bob* for you … charlie … people who don't know you *exist* … you can't get them off your *mind*!

Charlie That's b/cos they're cunts.

Toni They're not!

Charlie They are.

Toni They're just not like *you*!

Pause.

Charlie Well then they *must* be cunts.

Toni chuckles.

Toni Everything's a joke to you innit.

Charlie Listen tone. (*Pause.*) I love you.

Toni Bollocks.

Charlie It's true.

Toni So why didn't you show me?

Charlie I did … i mean i will … i wanted to … no-one

told me.

Toni Told you *what*?

Charlie This would happen.

Toni What?

Charlie This. (*Pause.*) I never thought it would happen.

Toni You mean you never thought it *could* happen … that's what you mean … you never thought that one day … someone might say …

Charlie I thought me and you was forever. (*Pause.*) Toni.

Toni That wasn't the deal.

Charlie We can still try.

Toni We can't.

Charlie Why not?

Toni It's too late.

Charlie It ain't … you know it ain't … it's only too late if you say it is.

Toni Well that's what i'm saying.

Charlie You can't be. (*Pause.*) I won't let you. (*Pause.*) Listen tone. (*Pause.*) I know i fucked up.

Toni We both did.

Charlie No i did.

Toni No … we both did … i fucked up as much as you.

Charlie Did you?

Toni nods.

Toni In different ways.

Charlie Well then we can fix it.

Toni shakes her head.

We can.

Toni shakes her head.

Look at this. (*He shows Toni his watch.*) What is it?

Toni looks bemused.

Toni It's your watch.

Charlie Look at it.

Toni looks at it.

Toni What about it?

Charlie It's still running!

Toni looks bemused.

Toni So?

Charlie How long have i had it?

Toni shrugs.

Toni Since i've known you.

Charlie Exactly! (*Pause.*) I went to wales this weekend.

Toni looks surprised.

Toni Did you?

Charlie Yeah.

Toni Where?

Charlie Brecon beacons.

Toni How come?

Charlie I wanted to clear my head. (*He taps his temple* *with his finger.*) Have a think ... you know ... that kinda shit.

Toni looks surprised.

Toni Really?

Charlie nods.

Charlie Unbelievable innit.

Toni With who?

Charlie Lee.

Toni shrugs.

Pukka lee ... guess what he said to me?

Toni How should i know?

Charlie He said i should get a new one. (*He shows Toni his watch.*)

Toni Why?

Charlie He said it was bust ... silly cunt ... he said it was bust ... but it weren't ... it had only *stopped* ... see ... i forgot to wind it. (*He shows Toni his watch.*) Look at it. (*He puts his watch up to Toni's ear.*) Purrs like a dream.

Toni So what?

Charlie *He* should fucking get a new one ... *he's* the cunt who fucked up and wants babies and flies fucking kites all day i mean no wonder jane's gone and left him!

Toni looks bemused.

Toni Who's jane?

Charlie His girlfriend ... she left him for roger ... it's complicated.

Toni You're telling me.

Charlie He thinks it's cos he's loaded but it ain't.

Toni What is it?

Charlie It's cos he's a fucking sap! (*He taps his temple with his finger.*) Soft in the head ... that's what it is ... believe.

Toni Charlie i give up on you.

Charlie You're damn right.

Toni chuckles.

Come here.

Toni shakes her head. Charlie walks up to her and takes her hand.

Toni No. (*She pulls it away.*)

Charlie What?

Toni I don't wanna.

Charlie Why not?

Toni B/cos you take me for granted.

Charlie I don't.

Toni You do ... you think you can waltz in ... any time ... sweep me off my feet. (*She shakes her head.*) Well not now.

Charlie What about tomorrow?

Toni looks at Charlie wearily.

I'm sorry. (*Pause.*) You look nice.

Pause.

Toni Thanks.

Charlie That a new dress?

Toni nods.

Where dya get it?

Toni In town.

Charlie nods.

Charlie You going out?

Toni Yeah.

Charlie Where?

Toni Pictures.

Charlie With who?

Pause.

Toni Charlie don't start.

Charlie I'm not.

Toni You are.

Pause.

Charlie Alright. (*Pause.*) You look nice tone.

Toni Thanks.

Pause.

Charlie You meeting your doctor? (*Pause.*) You are aren't you? (*Pause.*) Shit.

Pause.

Toni Charlie …

Charlie How can you go out with him?

Toni What's wrong with him?

Charlie He's a cunt.

Toni How would *you* know?

Charlie He just is … he wears a white coat and a stethoscope … it ain't happening. (*Pause.*) Dya know what i mean?

Toni No.

Charlie I mean … what i mean is … you can do better. (*He indicates himself.*) *Now* dya know what i mean?

Toni chuckles.

Toni Maybe.

Charlie Maybe what?

Pause.

Charlie and Toni Maybe baby.

They smile at each other. Charlie forwards the CD to the song 'I'll Be There For You'. He looks at Toni.

Charlie Remember this one?

Toni nods. Charlie turns the volume up and starts dancing in his own inimitable way. Toni watches him. Charlie beckons her to join him.

Come on.

Charlie closes his eyes and gets lost in the music. Toni watches him. Eventually she puts on her shoes and coat and walks off. Charlie is oblivious.
Blackout.

SCENE FOUR

N6. Kelly's bedroom. Thursday. 12.00 p.m. Paul Weller in the background. The futon is as a sofa. Charlie is sprawled across it. Kelly walks on with clean bedding.

Kelly Charlie.

Charlie What?

Kelly Get off.

Charlie Why?

Kelly I wanna make the bed.

Pause.

Charlie What's for breakfast?

Kelly looks bemused.

Kelly It's midnight.

Charlie So?

Kelly You're so cheeky.

Charlie I'm just curious.

Kelly sighs.

Come here.

Kelly No.

Charlie Come here. (*He beckons Kelly towards him.*)

Kelly Why?

Charlie I wanna ask you something.

Kelly drops the bedding and sits beside him.

Kelly What?

Charlie holds Kelly's face and kisses

What is it?

Charlie Are you my mate?

Kelly looks bemused.

Kelly What?

Charlie Are you?

Kelly No.

Charlie looks surprised.

Charlie Why not?

Kelly B/cos i don't *need* any mates ... i've got enough mates already.

Charlie Yeah but none like me.

Kelly raises her eyebrows.

Kelly What's so special about you?

Charlie smiles.

Charlie Don't you know?

Kelly No.

Charlie I'm a sweetheart.

Kelly smirks.

Kelly What?

Charlie Lee said.

Kelly When?

Charlie In wales.

Kelly He thinks you're a prat.

...rlie looks affronted.

Charlie What?

Kelly He told me.

Pause.

Charlie What a cunt.

Kelly Why dya say that?

Charlie What?

Kelly That word.

Charlie What word?

Kelly 'Cunt'. (*Pause.*) Why dya say it so much?

Charlie B/cos there's lots of em about.

Kelly sighs.

Kelly Now come on.

Charlie What?

Kelly Charlie!

Charlie What?

Kelly Get off!

Pause.

Charlie What's for breakfast?

Kelly drags Charlie off the futon with all her might. They laugh. Kelly lowers the futon into a bed and puts on the sheet and duvet.

Kelly There you can lie down now.

Charlie lies down on the futon. Kelly dims the light and picks up the pillows.

Dya wanna see some photos? (*Pause.*) Charlie.

Charlie What?

Kelly Dya wanna see some photos?

Charlie Of what?

Kelly Me.

Charlie No.

> *Kelly throws the pillows at Charlie.*

Oi!

> *Kelly laughs.*

What are they?

Kelly Me when i was small.

> *Charlie looks unenthusiastic.*

Charlie Go on then.

> *Kelly walks off and returns with a box. It is larger than Charlie expected. He looks startled.*

What's that!?

Kelly Pictures.

> *Charlie groans. Kelly sits beside Charlie and pulls out a photo.*

That's me and my sister.

Charlie Which one's you?

> *Kelly points.*

I like your sister.

> *Kelly hits Charlie.*

Oi! (*He nurses himself.*) That hurt!

Kelly Good. (*She pulls out a photo.*) That's me on my own. (*She pulls out a photo.*) That's me when i was five.

Charlie Ahh.

Kelly laughs.

You looked nice then.

Kelly motions to hit Charlie. He cowers.

I mean you look nice *now*!

Kelly pulls out a photo.

Kelly That's me and my mum.

Charlie Where's that?

Kelly Corfu.

Charlie Who's that fella?

Kelly John.

Charlie Who's he?

Kelly Her boyfriend.

Charlie looks at the photo.

Charlie What's he like?

Kelly shrugs.

Kelly He's alright.

Charlie Does he … ?

Pause.

Kelly What?

Charlie You know …

Pause.

Kelly What?

Charlie Kiss you?

Kelly looks bemused.

Kelly What?

Charlie When he goes to work.

Kelly No ... why?

Charlie Nothing ... it's just ... i know this girl ...

Kelly Young woman.

Charlie looks bemused.

Charlie What? (*Pause.*) Yeah.

Kelly Who is she?

Charlie She's just a girl.

Kelly sighs.

Anyhow she's got this thing about her stepdad ... well he's not her *real* stepdad anyway ... he kisses her and she kisses him and it's all very cosy but she don't like it.

Kelly I'm not surprised.

Charlie What ... ? No you don't get it ... he's just being friendly.

Kelly How dya know?

Charlie B/cos i know ... i told her ... it's all above board.

Kelly So?

Pause.

Charlie People always think the worst of people.

Kelly No they don't.

Charlie They do ... i mean alright he's a bit of cunt ... he wears pyjamas and that but ... at least he *tries* ... i mean it ain't easy being a mum's boyfriend ... i told her ... specially these days ... but he does his best ... he could fuck about doing nothing but he don't.

Kelly Don't he?

Charlie No ... he makes things.

Kelly What things?

Charlie French windows.

Kelly Does he?

Charlie nods.

Charlie He did some for the lounge ... he looked at the lounge and he thought ... 'i know ... i'll do some french windows ... lovely' ... and that's what he did ... but the thing is he didn't just stop there ... he didn't just stand back and gaze at his windows ... no ... he went and started on the floorboards ... lovely shiny floorboards they got ... mustard ... i could do with some myself ... better than allied carpets.

Kelly Charlie.

Charlie What?

Kelly looks bemused.

Kelly What are you *on* about?

Charlie I'm just saying ...

Kelly looks at Charlie inquiringly.

Are you my mate?

Kelly Charlie!

Charlie I'm saying ... everyone's different ... that's all ...

they wear wigs or they wear pyjamas or they go bloody
hang gliding …

Kelly Hang gliding?

Charlie Yeah. But that don't mean they're cunts.

Kelly I never said it did.

Charlie It means … they're not like *you* … that's what it
means.

Kelly looks bemused.

Kelly You don't make sense.

Charlie chuckles ruefully.

Charlie I know … i never do.

Kelly looks bemused.

Toni says.

Kelly raises her eyebrows.

Kelly Really?

Charlie nods.

What else does she say?

Charlie Hey?

Kelly looks at Charlie inquiringly.

Why dya wanna know?

Kelly I don't.

Charlie looks bemused.

I don't *care* what she says.

Charlie I know.

Kelly She's not my *problem.*

Charlie So?

Kelly She's yours. (*Pause.*) Talk about her with your mates.

Charlie smiles.

Charlie You *are* my mate.

Kelly I'm not … i told you … i don't *wanna* be your mate … mates are different.

Charlie How?

Kelly They just are … if you wanna talk about her go.

Charlie What?

Kelly Go.

Pause.

Charlie You don't mean it.

Kelly I do. (*Pause.*) I'm not here to comfort you charlie.

Charlie I know.

Pause.

Kelly I want you to go.

Pause.

Charlie Shit. (*He shakes his head in wonder.*) Not again … everywhere i go i get kicked out. (*He reluctantly puts on his shoes. He pecks Kelly on the cheek.*) See ya later. (*He walks towards the door. He turns to face Kelly.*) Kelly.

Kelly What?

Charlie It's midnight.

Kelly So?

Pause.

Charlie It's cold outside.

Kelly I don't care.

Charlie spots Kelly's jumper.

Charlie Let me borrow your jumper.

Kelly No.

Charlie takes Kelly's jumper.

I said no.

Charlie I'll give ya it tomorrow.

Kelly shakes her head.

Why not?

Kelly I won't see you tomorrow.

Pause.

Charlie Saturday then.

Kelly shakes her head.

Sunday.

Kelly shakes her head.

I'll put it in the post.

Kelly shakes her head. Charlie walks up to Kelly and offers her the jumper.

Take it.

Kelly takes the jumper.

You're a hard woman.

Kelly I have to be.

Charlie Why?

Kelly You know why.

Charlie shakes his head.

I don't wanna see you if you're thinking of toni.

Charlie I'm not.

Kelly You are.

Charlie I'm thinking of *you*.

Kelly looks at Charlie dubiously.

And toni. (*He taps his temple with his finger.*) I can think of lots of things ... i'm good like that.

Kelly chuckles.

I'll tell ya what.

Kelly looks at Charlie inquiringly.

I'll only think of you from now on. (*He holds Kelly's head up.*) Okay? (*Pause.*) What dya say? (*He sits beside Kelly and pulls out a photo.*) What's that?

Kelly smiles at the photo.

Kelly That's me and my dog ... boris ... he's dead now.

Charlie Is he?

Kelly nods.

Kelly He died when i was twelve poor thing ... don't you think he's lovely?

Charlie He's a sensation.

Kelly hits Charlie.

What!?

Kelly pulls out a glossy black-and-white print.

Who's that?

Kelly Glenn hoddle.

Charlie Who?

Kelly Glenn hoddle.

Charlie shrugs.

Don't you know glenn hoddle?

Charlie No.

Kelly He's a footballer.

Charlie I can see that … so?

Kelly He was my hero.

Charlie Was he?

Kelly gazes at the photo.

Kelly He's gorgeous.

Charlie looks at the photo.

Charlie I dunno. (*Pause.*) I never knew you liked football?

Kelly nods.

Kelly I've always liked it.

Charlie How come?

Kelly My dad used to take me.

Charlie Did he?

Kelly nods.

When?

Kelly When i was a kid.

Charlie Why did he stop?

Kelly shrugs.

Kelly He just did. (*Pause.*) A lot of things stopped when he left.

Charlie Did they?

Kelly nods.

He don't have to take you.

Kelly I know … but i like going with someone.

Charlie Do you?

Kelly nods.

I'll take you.

Kelly looks surprised.

Kelly But you don't like football.

Charlie So?

Kelly smiles.

Kelly You're sweet. (*She kisses Charlie on the lips.*)

Charlie Are you my mate?

Kelly shakes her head.

Don't lie.

Kelly I'm not.

Charlie looks disappointed.

So football's not your forte?

Charlie shakes his head.

Charlie Nah.

Kelly What is?

Charlie Helicopters.

Kelly looks bemused.

Kelly What?

Charlie Aeroplanes.

Kelly looks bemused.

Kelly What?

Charlie ponders.

Charlie Fish and chips.

Kelly looks bemused. She pulls out a photo.

Kelly That's me and my nan in cambridge. (*She pulls out a photo.*) That's me when i had plaits look. (*She pulls out a photo.*) That's me and siobhan ... she lived across the road ... i was in *love* with her brother. (*She gazes at the photo.*) Christ. (*She pulls out a photo.*) That's me. (*She pulls out a photo.*) That's me. (*She pulls out a photo.*) That's me. (*She pulls out a photo.*) That's me. (*She pulls out a photo.*)

Charlie That's not you is it?

Kelly Yeah.

They laugh. Kelly pulls out a photo.

Charlie Kelly.

Kelly looks at Charlie inquiringly.

Kelly What?

Charlie Dya think we could we do this later?

Kelly looks disappointed.

Kelly Okay. (*She stands and starts undressing.*)

Charlie What are you doing?

Kelly stops undressing.

Kelly What dya think? (*Pause.*) Undressing.

Charlie Why?

Kelly I wanna go to bed. (*Pause.*) What's the matter?

Charlie Nothing.

Kelly What is it?

Pause.

Charlie Nothing.

Pause.

Kelly What?

Pause.

Charlie Listen kelly i don't know you.

Kelly So?

Pause.

Charlie So this is nice ... but it can't happen.

Kelly What can't?

Charlie Me and you.

Kelly So why don't you go?

Pause.

Charlie What?

Kelly Why don't you go?

Pause.

Charlie B/cos you won't lend me your jumper.

Kelly picks up the jumper and offers it to Charlie.

Kelly Take it.

Charlie takes the jumper.

See ya later. (*She walks towards the door.*)

Charlie Where you going?

Kelly To brush my teeth.

Charlie Can't we do that together?

Kelly walks off. Pause. Charlie looks at the jumper. He puts it on. It feels small. He pulls it off. Pause. He unties his laces and starts pulling off his shoes.
Blackout.